365 TIPS AND IDEAS FOR IMPROVING YOUR SKILLS AND CREATIVITY

A Watercolour
a Day

Óscar Asensio

promopress

A Watercolour a Day.
365 Tips and Ideas from Improving your Skills and Creativity

Author: Óscar Asensio
Design and layout: Michael Sorin
Editor: Andrea Korniusza
Translator: Gwenydd Jones
Cover design: spread: David Lorente
Cover images: Front: The lynx by Alarie Tano. All the images selected from the pages of this book

Editorial development
Línea Editorial

ISBN: 978-84-16504-89-3
D.L.: B-12-2018

Promopress is a registered trademark of:
Promotora de prensa internacional S.A.
C/ Ausiàs March 124
08013 Barcelona, Spain.
Tel.: 0034 93 245 14 64
Fax: 0034 93 265 48 83
Email: info@promopress.es
www.promopresseditions.com
Facebook: Promopress Editions
Twitter: Promopress Editions @PromopressEd

First edition in English: 2018

Printed in Malaysia

Index

INTRODUCTION 4

MATERIALS 8

COLOUR AND WATERCOLOUR 28

DRY AND WET TECHNIQUES 52

GOUACHE 106

WATERCOLOURS BY SUBJECT 122

    Landscapes 123

    Marine art 132

    Nudes 139

    Fruit 146

    Animals 154

    Flowers 161

    Portraits 168

CONTRIBUTOR INDEX 174

FURTHER READING 176

Introduction

WHAT IS WATERCOLOUR PAINTING?

———

The term watercolour is a compound noun formed by the words *water* and *colour*. The dictionary defines it as "painting produced using colours diluted in water". There is nothing coincidental or random about this definition.

Water is the medium that allows the artist to transfer the features and qualities of the colour of different pigments to paper. These pigments have been diluted and bound using other substances, like gum arabic, which is made of Senegal gum or talah gum, to name a couple. Purists working with the watercolour technique will often add other components to their paint. These include glycerine, honey, ox gall and preservative agents, such as phenol and sodium orthophenylphenate. These solutions are known as tints. When the artist adds a medium to the paper using a brush or another tool, they are performing a wash.

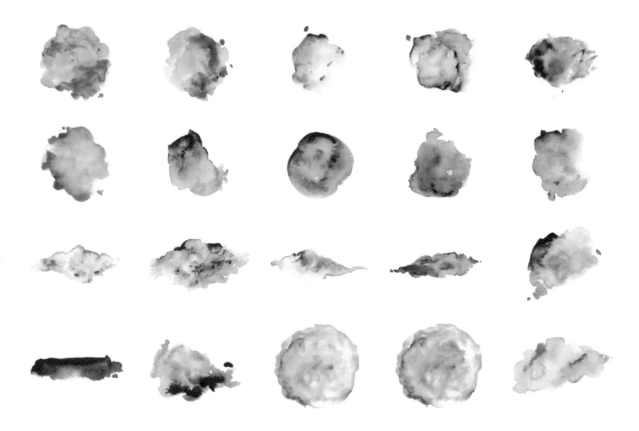

THE IMPORTANCE OF COLOUR IN WATERCOLOUR PAINTING

Watercolour paints are created by forming a compound of dry pigments, in dust form, mixed with gum arabic. These paints are soluble in water. In practice, the artist will normally dissolve pre-preprepared paint in distilled water and apply it to paper using a paintbrush. The salient characteristic of watercolour paintings is the transparency generated by these diluted pigments.

Watercolour painting has been extremely popular since the late 19th century. The technique's enormous popularity is what led it to lose a certain amount of prestige. This was the consequence of watercolour painting being primarily associated with the higher strata of society, whose members transformed their love of painting into an enjoyable pastime. Hobbyists would use watercolours as their means of expression, repeatedly producing delicate landscapes, where pastel tones prevailed.

WHY IS WATER AT THE HEART OF THIS TECHNIQUE?

Water is the protagonist in watercolour painting. It is the reason for this technique's signature transparency and luminance, two characteristics that are almost impossible to achieve with any other medium.

Watercolour painting involves combining water with a small quantity of pigment. Once the water has evaporated, this pigment is deposited, forming a translucent layer.

This is what allows the white of the paper to remain visible underneath the paint, providing the transparent quality typical of a good watercolour painting.

▲
Snowfall in Guitiriz, **Manuel Gandullo**

WHY IS IT THE MOST ADMIRED TECHNIQUE?

————

Artworks produced using this technique undergo an interesting transformation. It involves changing from a highly vivid appearance, when the paint is wet, to taking on a more subdued, lighter aspect, once it is dry. This transformation, which clearly changes the appearance of the final work, may involve the colour lightening up to as much as 50%, depending on the quantity of paint used to charge the brush when producing the watercolour. For the artist to achieve the appearance they want, it is essential they remember this process while producing their work.

Even though some purists may say there is a correct way of painting with watercolours, meaning a way that 'respects' norms established in times gone by, nowadays, an increasing number of artists use and combine different techniques in the same work, in pursuit of a certain result.

◄ *The entrance,*
Ali Cavanaugh

WHY DO WE LIKE PAINTING WITH WATERCOLOURS?

The watercolour technique is the most popular among people wanting to take their first steps in the fine art of painting. Experts will often consider it the most complex technique, but this is precisely one of the aspects that make it the most interesting. The artist can use watercolours to produce vivid paintings. It is a popular technique for portraying landscapes and marine art, and the best way of depicting water. The fusion between the different colours, which results from their water content, confers a beauty on the final work that cannot be achieved using other techniques. The light in the painting, once the artist is advanced, is radiant and powerful, regardless of the technique they employ. The medium the artist uses as their canvas to paint their watercolour also gives them an unrivalled advantage. They will normally use paper with a medium or rough grain, which gives the artwork a strong plastic quality. These factors combined make watercolour the most appealing painting technique.

WHY A WATERCOLOUR A DAY?

If there is one point that every therapist in the world will agree on, it is that a good way of relieving daily stress is to paint. Painting is slowly being transformed from a hobby into a therapy, with surprising results for people who dedicate a little time to it every day, whether they be children, young people or adults. For professional watercolourists, painting every day is an activity that allows them to properly develop their skills and creativity. *A Watercolour a Day* gives you 365 pointers and tips, illustrated through works by more than 70 world-renowned artists. In the pages of this book, you will get to know the materials you need and how to use them correctly. You will find guidelines for painting the most popular subjects, pointers on managing the technique effectively, and tips on how to continue improving. In short, this book will give you all the tools you need to have fun and disconnect through the art of painting.

Dream, **Ayşe Eylül Sönmez**
▼

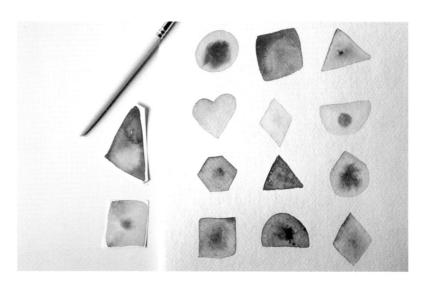

Materials

Materials play an extremely important role when you paint a watercolour. This chapter discusses the essential materials and tools for performing the watercolour technique. It will also show you how to look after your tools, to make sure you keep them in good working order over time.

1
CHEMISTRY IN WATERCOLOURS

What most appeals about painting with watercolours is the transparency of the colours, which will make your painting look fresh, luminous and spontaneous. Watercolour paint was designed to be used with water, and to be applied to paper. Despite this, nowadays, artists produce watercolours on different media, including cardboard and clay.

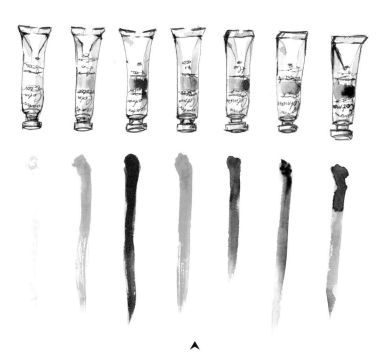

2
COMPOSITION OF WATERCOLOUR PAINT

Watercolour paint is a mixture of powdered natural pigments and binding substances, like gum arabic, which convert the powder into a mass.

Before starting a watercolour, it is important to select appropriate colours to use. If you are a beginner, it is easier to use a smaller colour palette.

Different pigments will dye the medium to a greater or lesser extent.

3

PIGMENTS

Pigments are small particles that create colour. Each pigment has a specific origin, which means they react differently. They may have a greater or lesser ability to dye the medium. Some are transparent in nature, while others are slightly opaque. This is why the artist has to be very careful when selecting the colour combination they are going to use in their composition.

4

INORGANIC PIGMENTS

These pigments are derived from compounds that were never part of living material. They do not contain carbon. This group includes cadmiums, cobalt, ultramarine, earth tones and an extensive range of other traditional colours.

How liquid watercolour looks when it is in a special container for this type of paint.

ORGANIC PIGMENTS

Pigments of this type are derived from living substances, or substances that used to be part of something living. This group includes numerous modern pigments that are known for their clarity and transparency. Examples include phthalocyanine, quinacridone, perylene and benzimidazolone. These pigments contain carbon.

Watercolour paint is also available in tubes.

SINGLE PIGMENTS

All pigments differ in shape, size, colour and nature. Pigments, particularly in watercolour paint, are the toolbox or elements that allow the artist to 'speak'. They are what helps them manipulate their artwork and alter how it is expressed. That is why many brands try to create formulas based on single pigments. A formula that contains a single pigment will have a purer tone and cleaner colour than one based on a pigment blend. This will help the artist mix a wider range of colours, and delay the appearance of the effects of blotting.

Permanent alizarin crimson.

Hooker's green.

MIXED PIGMENTS

Though mixed pigments will inevitably lose some of their chromatic intensity or vividness, there are numerous reasons why brands like Winston & Newton still use them in their formulas. In some cases, you can achieve a superior level of permanence using a mixed pigment, such as permanent alizarin crimson and Hooker's green. In others, several pigments have to be mixed to achieve a certain formula. This is the case with quinacridone gold, whose pigment is no longer available.

NATURAL EARTH PIGMENTS

Earth pigments are the oldest type of colouring material in the world. In the caves of Altamira and Lascaux, you can find artworks created using them at least 15,000 years ago. Natural earth pigments are essential in watercolour painting owing to their low colouring strength and natural tones. They are also essential, because you cannot obtain them by mixing black or white tones. Earth pigments are colour deposits that have normally acquired their tone as a result of having been in contact with iron for millions of years. They are some of the most inert and permanent pigments you will find. Earth pigments are extracted from the ground and subsequently washed and cleaned.

◀ *A painting produced entirely using earth tones.*

SYNTHETIC EARTH PIGMENTS

Synthetic earth pigments comprise the group of pigments that has replaced natural earth pigments due to their lack of availability. They are synthetic iron oxides. These pigments are attractive in and of themselves, since they tend to be quite resistant and opaque. The earliest examples date back to the mid-19th century. Though synthetic iron oxides offer good specifications, they do not completely replace earth pigments. Consequently, the artist would be well advised to keep a stock of natural and synthetic earth pigments.

ALTERNATIVE PIGMENTS

As mentioned earlier, cadmiums are the most popular reds and yellows in the palette. When sold as artist's paint and used normally, they represent no danger to the user's health. Despite this, there has been public concern about the cadmium compounds used in other industries, and their impact on the environment. Taking this into account, artists who can do without the singular characteristics of cadmiums may opt to use alternatives. There are no direct substitutes for these tones, but options are available that share some of their features.

CADMIUM PIGMENTS

Paints containing cadmium pigments represent an important colour range in the artist's palette. Their singular tones, good coverage and low colouring strength are qualities no other pigment available can equal. What is more, they have excellent solidity in light and are highly opaque. These are the most popular reds and yellows in the artist's palette.

Cadmium yellow.

Cadmium red.

◄ *Shy,*
Alarie Tano

12

QUINACRIDONES

This is a very important pigment group, created in the 1950s. The first quinacridones were introduced by Winsor & Newton, and included permanent pink and permanent magenta. The high transparency and solidity in light of these colours led them to transform the pink and mauve section of the palette, an area that had always been singled out as lacking solidity in light. With time, it became possible to make numerous other tones available in this range.

13

TRANSPARENCY AND OPACITY

Transparency is the key feature of watercolour paint. The finer the layer of paint, the better. As a result of this feature, the colours will look transparent on the paper. This also allows the brilliance of the paper's reflective white to come through. However, it is important that the pigments have the ability to maintain their natural characteristics, to a certain degree. For instance, transparent pigments reflect light in a similar way to fused glass, creating metallic gleams and clean mixtures. Opaque colours, like the cadmiums, will probably provide much more coverage than transparent ones. The different transparency and opacity of a pigment will affect how an individual colour looks, and how the tone blends with others. More transparent colours will let the artist create a pure glazed effect, by applying a series of overlaid washes. More opaque colours produce flatter washes and provide greater coverage over previous applications. They are also useful for softening mixed colours.

GRANULATION

Some pigments have a characteristic called granulation. Granulation refers to when the particles in a pigment settle on the paper and give rise to a speckled effect. For many artists, granulation is a highly attractive quality, since it incorporates visual texture into their paintings. Different paints with granulation create different effects when the artist brushes them onto the paper. Some finer pigments group together, in a process known as flocculation, while other heavier pigments find their way into the pores on the surface of the paper. As a general rule, traditional pigments—such as cobalts, earths and ultramarine—demonstrate granulation, while the more modern organic ones do not have this characteristic. To avoid granulation in your paintings, try using distilled water. This can reduce it, particularly if you live in an area with hard water.

▲
Example of brush-strokes forming granulation in a painting.

PRUSSIAN BLUE DYE

The stability of watercolour paint depends on the relative absorbency of the surface of the paper. Due to this characteristic, stronger colours—like Prussian blue, alizarin crimson and modern organic pigments—created using very fine particles, will penetrate or dye the paper more than other colours. These paints cannot be completely removed using a damp sponge. Traditional inorganic colours and earth tones are normally easier to remove from the paper.

This image shows two tones of the colour Prussian blue. ▶

16

REMOVING A COLOUR

To eliminate or remove a colour, you have to lift it off the paper using a sponge. You can also remove it by washing the entire watercolour under running water. A sponge can also serve as a technical tool, to create a 'smoky' background, for instance. As another alternative, you can buy specially formulated products for lifting the paint. Winsor & Newton paint removal solution is one example. It makes it easy to remove paints from the paper, even ones that dye it, using a damp sponge or brush. After applying removal solution to the paper, leave the area to dry before you paint over it again. The stability of watercolour paint depends on the relative absorbency of the surface of the paper. Due to this characteristic, stronger colours—like Prussian blue, alizarin crimson and modern organic pigments—created using very fine particles, will penetrate or dye the paper more than other colours. These paints cannot be completely removed using a damp sponge. Traditional inorganic colours and earth tones are normally easier to remove from the paper.

Image showing the gum arabic used to manufacture watercolour paint.

17

GUM ARABIC

This is one of the main components of watercolour paint and its function is to bind the pigments.

18

BINDERS

A binder is mixed with the pigment to produce the paint. Its purpose is to help the pigment stick to the paper or other medium. Gum arabic is the most popular binder for creating watercolour paints, but it is not the only one.

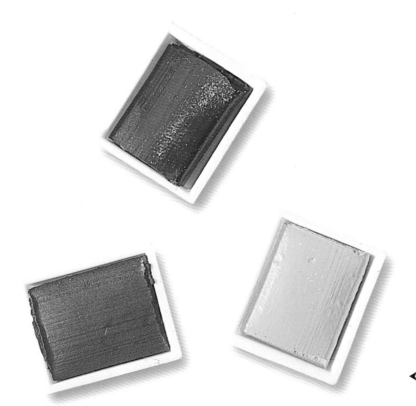

DRY WATERCOLOUR PAINT

This type of watercolour paint is available on the market in tablet or cake form, also known as pans. These solid paints have to be dampened in order to use the colour. They are normally sold in boxes that contain palettes with an assortment of colours, or as individual pans, by colour.

◄ *Pans containing three pure colours in their initial state.*

20

WATERCOLOUR PASTE

This is sold in tubes. Unlike with pans, the paint is sold as a paste because it contains more humectants, which means it dries more slowly. You can buy tubes individually or in assorted boxes. The main advantage of the paste format is that it lets you mix colours without dirtying one with the other.

Dry watercolours are one variety of the paint used in this technique. ▶

Format for liquid watercolour paint.

LIQUID WATERCOLOUR PAINT

This format is presented in flasks or bottles. It is most suitable for painting techniques involving flat (uniform) colours. In fact, this format of watercolour paint is more frequently used in graphic design and illustration than in artistic painting. These paints are transparent, with exceptional brilliance and luminosity. What is more, they do not contain pigments and can be immediately mixed together You can dilute them with water and they create no deposits. Among other products, liquid watercolour paint is ideal for use in airbrushing, since it is completely water soluble and contains no additives that could obstruct the valve of the apparatus.

22

WATERCOLOUR MEDIUM

This is a mixture of gum arabic, acetic acid and water. For painting, it is used dissolved in water. A few drops per half litre are sufficient to remove traces of grease, create greater intensity, brilliance and transparency, and improve adherence. In general terms, you can use this product to thicken the paint. To do this, mix the medium directly with the paint.

Prepare the paper to get better results in your painting. ➤

OX GALL

This is a refined substance that alters the surface tension of the water, which means the paint will dry in an average time. Consequently, if used in winter, the paint will dry more quickly, while in summer, drying time will be longer. You can add it to the water you are using or mix it directly with the paint. It also improves the fluidity and adherence of the paint.

VARNISHES

These are used to protect the colours and make them shine slightly. You can buy varnish as a liquid, to be applied using a brush, or in aerosol format. When applied with a brush, it is essential to make sure you do this once the watercolour is completely dry, to avoid dragging the paint, which could dirty another colour in your artwork. Overusing varnish can impoverish and mask the tones. This issue primarily affects lighter and paler tones, where you could end up distorting the main effect.

LIQUID GUM OR MASKING FLUID

This is a creamy solution made of natural latex and ammonia. The artist brushes it onto the paper and it creates an impermeable film, which protects the paper from the paint. This way, they can block out parts of the paper and keep them blank, to suggest brightness and sparkle, or objects that are white in colour. Block-out gum can be easily removed from the paper by rubbing it lightly with your finger or an eraser. Despite this, it is better not to leave liquid gum on the paper for long periods of time, since it could become too firmly attached and ruin the paper when you try to remove it. To apply this substance, it is best to use an old paintbrush, since the gum may damage the hairs. You could use a dip pen, if the part you want to block out is a fine line or small detail.

Masking fluid, also known as liquid gum, can be applied using a brush. It is used to block out the desired areas.

SALT

This element is used to achieve original textures and effects. To obtain them, you have to place salt on top of the wash.

GLYCERIN

This is used to delay drying. You have to put a small amount in the water container. Artists will normally use it on windy or very warm days. It can come in handy when painting using a wet watercolour technique.

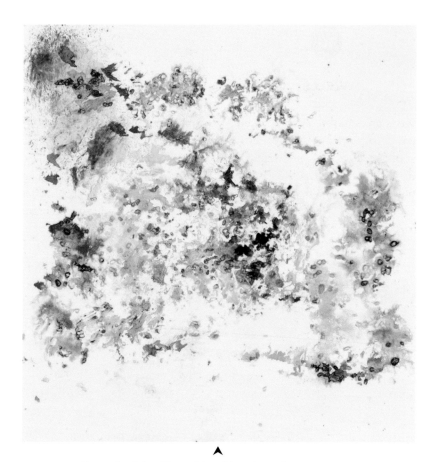

Example of the effect achieved by using salt on a painting.

ALCOHOL

Unlike glycerin, alcohol is used to accelerate drying. It is frequently used on very cold or damp days, or in any other circumstance where the artist wants their painting to dry more quickly. It is essential to always use pure 96° alcohol.

WATER JARS

Use these to hold the liquid you will employ to dissolve your watercolours. Jars also serve to clean your paintbrushes every time you change colour. It is important that the jar has the capacity to hold at least half a litre. This is because, in smaller flasks, the paint content becomes too dense and the water gets dirty quickly.

Water is an extremely important element when painting with watercolours.

WELLS

Wells are small recipients where you dissolve the paint in water to achieve a specific tone that you do not want to vary during application.

MIXING PALETTES

These are trays that contain cells where you can keep the paint, to use and prepare it. You will find a wide range of types and sizes. Some place greater importance on the palette, and others on the cells. They normally offer a combination of round and rectangular cells, since this can be useful for playing with paint density. The round ones are designed to hold paint with a higher water content, while the rectangular ones are more suited to paste.

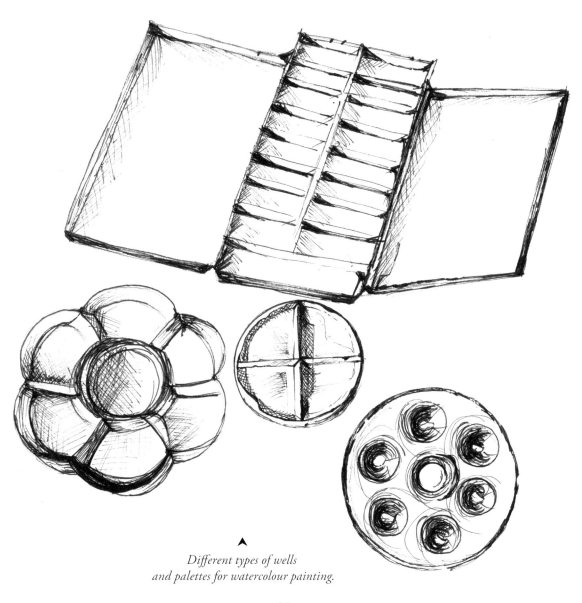

▲
Different types of wells
and palettes for watercolour painting.

21

PALETTES

This is the tool the artist uses to mix colours. Palettes are made of, or coated in, water-repellent materials. The paint should slip off them easily. They may have a hole, where you can put your thumb, to help you hold onto them. They are normally made of enamelled metal, ceramic or plastic, and coloured white, to avoid distorting the colours.

Besides being designed to store paint, this box can also be used to mix colours.

PAPER

The history of watercolour painting is intimately linked to the history of paper. It is an important product, and one that has accompanied, and been used to keep records of, the development of numerous societies and cultures throughout the world.

DIFFERENT TYPES OF WATERCOLOUR PAPER

Nowadays, you can buy paper from a wide variety of brands and with different specifications for painting with watercolours. Watercolour paper is categorised based on its weight or thickness. The weight of paper is based on the weight of a ream (i.e. 500 sheets).

DIFFERENT PAPER GRAMMAGES

The most typical grammages for watercolour papers are: 185 g/m², 200 g/m², 240 g/m², 250 g/m², 280 g/m², 300 g/m², 350 g/m², 356 g/m², 650 g/m² and 850 g/m². But, there are many types of paper with special characteristics, such as torchon paper, which, instead of having a defined grain, has wider, shallower undulations.

USING WATERCOLOUR PAPER

Most watercolour papers can be used on both sides, bearing in mind that one will be more granulated than the other. You can buy papers that are cold-pressed or hot-pressed.

HOT-PRESSED PAPER

Hot-pressed papers have a glossy, smooth surface which, when you use the watercolours, will not absorb the washes very well, creating an opaque or dirty appearance.

Before starting to paint with watercolours, it is important to choose the correct type of paper.

Basic materials for stretching the paper.

23

COLD-PRESSED PAPER

Cold-pressed paper has a surface with a very good texture for absorbing the water and letting it flow, which results in well-defined edges and outlines.

TEXTURES OF WATERCOLOUR PAPER

The grain or texture of the paper is a factor that determines the technique the artist uses and the effect of the painting. Irregularities in the grain give depth to the tone and colour of the painting. Medium and fine are the most used grains. More experienced watercolourists will sometimes prefer paper with a rough grain, particularly when painting floral subjects.

PREPARING THE PAPER

Part of the task of painting with watercolours relates to preparing the paper. Normally, if the weight of the paper is below 300 g, it will start buckling as soon as it comes into contact with water. One excellent solution is to use a support, preferably made of wood, to position and stretch the paper, so you can glide the pigment-charged brush over it freely.

Example of stretched paper.

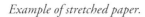

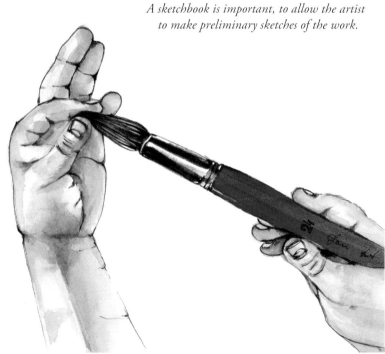

A sketchbook is important, to allow the artist to make preliminary sketches of the work.

USING A BOARD

Another option is to use a board and attach the paper to it with gummed paper tape, on all four edges. With this type of board, you paint directly onto the paper and, once the sheet is dry, you separate it from the board by easing a flat spatula into a small opening on one of the edges.

42

PAINTBRUSHES

Most painters who work with watercolours will do so using a paintbrush. These days, you will find an enormous variety of paintbrushes available on the market. In any case, note that you can complete an entire watercolour painting using just two or three brushes. From a position that may be judged somewhat extreme, purists maintain that a single brush is sufficient. While this may be true, it is only the case once the painter has become proficient. Only then will it be possible to use a single paintbrush to add precise details and delicate touches, like filling and producing background layers.

NATURAL-HAIR PAINTBRUSHES

These are the softest paintbrushes you can buy. They are made of natural hair from different animals, with sable hair being used to produce brushes of the highest quality. Sable hair is normally used to make watercolour brushes because the fibre is soft and it will hold more water and colour than a synthetic brush. There are lots of different types of sable paintbrush. You can also find paintbrushes made using the hair of other animals, like squirrels, goats and oxen, to name but a few.

Round natural-hair paintbrushes.

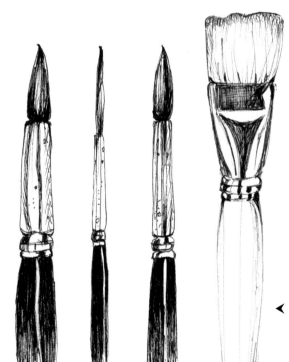

Paintbrushes come in numerous varieties. It is important to choose the right brush before you start your painting.

SYNTHETIC PAINTBRUSHES

These are made of nylon or polyester filaments. One of their main advantages is that these filaments can be altered in many different ways, to obtain softer, more porous or harder paintbrushes. These paintbrushes are economic alternatives to ones made of natural hair. They have medium absorbency, without achieving the levels of the kolinsky sable or squirrel. They release the pigment less gradually, have a feeling of firmness and mark an outline well. This is an acceptable alternative, although a synthetic filament has still not been produced that can equal all the properties of the finest natural hairs, like the kolinsky sable and the best of the red sable.

WHICH PAINTBRUSHES TO CHOOSE

Someone who has decided to learn how to paint with watercolours will need two or three types of paintbrush to get started. It is best to have a brush that will allow you to wash pigment over large areas of paper, another for medium-sized areas and finally, one for the details. The recommendation is two or three, since the same brush could be used for medium-sized areas and details. Remember that the brushes you use for watercolours should be soft. You should also bear in mind that the longer the hair, the more water the brush will absorb. Other desirable features are good resistance and elasticity, in addition to a high capacity for absorption. One way to identify whether a brush is absorbent or not is to dampen it and pass it over your thumbnail. When you do this, the hair should not drip, but slide, and then return to its original shape.

Flat synthetic-hair paintbrushes.

Colour and watercolour

Colour is an extremely important part of watercolour painting. Colours allow the artist to paint everything they want, with their imagination being their only limitation. The market currently offers approximately 120 different pigments for watercolour painting. Obviously, one artist is not going to buy all of them. In fact, just a few will suffice. This is because mixing certain tones will allow you to obtain others.

COLOUR

In reality, colour does not exist. Light exists, and colour is a result of it. However, our lives are surrounded by colours. These are more than just an expression, like sky blue, snow white or tomato red. In reality, our perception of blue, white or red, for instance, is no more than our eyes capturing a certain beam of light and our brains processing it. That is why we know colours do not exist, and that they are actually the result of the phenomenon of light reflection.

Coloured cans, **Hsin-I Kuo**

VARIABLES OF COLOUR

There are four basic variables that can intervene in and alter colours. These are hue, value or luminance, tone and saturation.

This image shows variables of basic tones when painting with watercolours.

 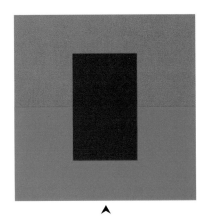 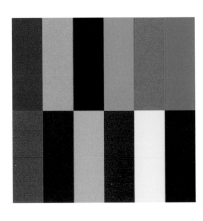

Hue is what allows us to distinguish red from blue, and refers to how colours are positioned on the colour wheel.

48

HUE

This refers to each of the gradations a colour may have without losing the name that distinguishes it from the others.

49

VALUE OR LUMINANCE

This is one intrinsic quality of colour. It indicates the degree of lightness or darkness a colour possesses. On the colour wheel, yellow is the colour with the highest luminance, while violet has the lowest. Colours can be altered by adding lighter colours. If you want to make a colour darker, you have to add portions of a complimentary colour, so it can decrease its luminance.

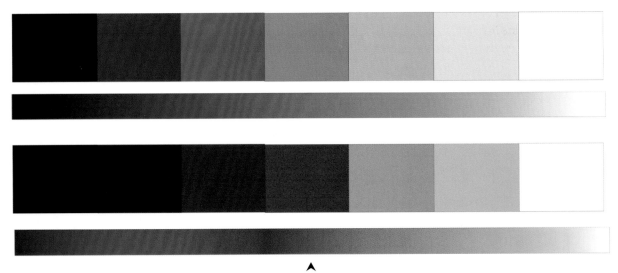

The value or luminance of a colour is what tells us its relative lightness or darkness.

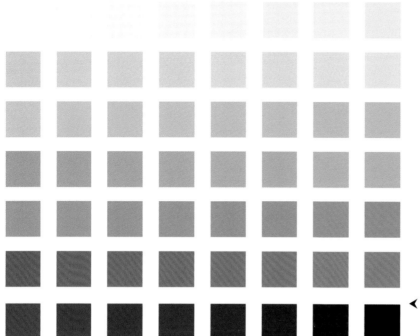

TONE

This refers to the result of mixing colours with white or black. This variable relates to hue and value. For instance, yellow mixed with black changes the hue towards green, and the colour gets darker.

◄ *Detail showing tones from black to white.*

51

SATURATION

This refers to the level of purity of a colour and is measured in relation to grey. Highly saturated colours have a high level of purity and become more intense as their value increases. Colours with lower saturation appear greyer, with more impurities and lower intensity.

Lively, **Hsin-I Kuo** ➤

SYMBOLOGY OF THE COLOUR RED

Red is the symbol of ardent, overflowing passion, of sexuality and eroticism.

The idea of summer, **Hsin-I Kuo**

After the rain, **Laurin McCracken**

SYMBOLOGY OF THE COLOUR ORANGE

Orange represents joy, youth, heat and summer.

SYMBOLOGY OF THE COLOUR YELLOW

In many cultures, yellow is the symbol of the deity and the brightest, warmest and most ardent and expansive colour.

Seven little ducks, **Hsin-I Kuo**

SYMBOLOGY OF THE COLOUR GREEN

Green is a symbol of hope, fertility, good things to come and the desire for eternal life. It represents nature.

Magic land, **Hsin-I Kuo**

Excessive,
Hsin-I Kuo

56

SYMBOLOGY OF THE COLOUR WHITE

White is associated with purity, faith and peace. It represents mystery.

57

SYMBOLOGY OF THE COLOUR PURPLE

Purple represents mystery.

Egg plants and bowls,
Laurin McCracken

58

SYMBOLOGY OF THE COLOUR BLUE

Blue symbolises depth.

Canning jars on black,
Laurin McCracken

SYMBOLOGY OF THE COLOUR BLACK

Black is traditionally related to darkness, pain, desperation, formality, solemnity, sadness, melancholy, unhappiness, misfortune, anger and irritability. It can also represent things that are hidden and veiled. The meaning of white is associated with purity, faith and peace. It represents mystery.

Farmer going home, **Hsin-I Kuo**

SYMBOLOGY OF THE COLOUR GREY

Grey equalises everything and does not influence the other colours.

Flat cans without colour, **Hsin-I Kuo**

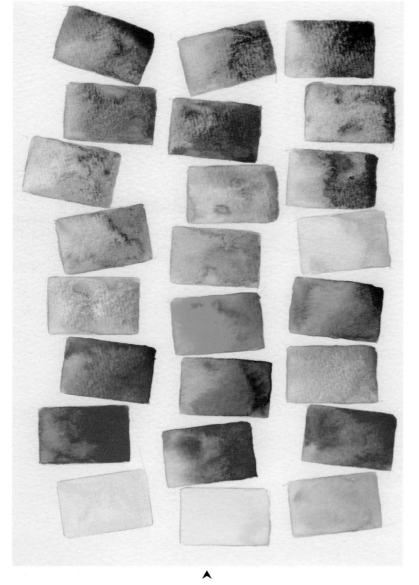

Example of a colour palette for painting with watercolours.

COLOUR PALETTES

A painter's palette should not be confused with the term colour palette. The first refers to a tool, the one the artist uses to hold their paint, so they can mix colours. Colour palette refers to the personal set of colours that each painter uses most frequently.

COOL COLOURS

Cool colours fall into the blue-green range. They are an essential part of the palette. French sea blue is a solid, basic blue. Cobalt blue is a more intense pigment. It is also a little lighter. A basic green is grass or meadow green. Leaf green is a little lighter. A good option for artists looking for a different tone is to try working with Prussian or thalo blue, which have a metallic or cobalt turquoise tinge. Including a violet, like mauve, is also an excellent option.

Basic assortment for a palette of cool colours.

Painting produced in its entirety using a palette of cool colours.

Basic assortment for a palette of warm colours.

WARM COLOURS

Warm colours are made up of colours that go from the yellow range to the red range. Cadmium tones are the strongest. They are also the most traditional. Cadmium yellow, cadmium red and cadmium orange are a good place to start. Vermilion is clear red in colour. It has a vibrant brilliance. Clear orange is also a good option because it combines very cleanly with white.

Painting produced in its entirety using a palette of warm colours.

BLACK AND WHITE

Black and white are both essential colours in your palette. This is because, while they should not be applied directly, you will need them to create different nuances and neutral mixtures. Titanium white is the standard white used. Chinese white is softer. Standard black has a warmness to it.

The killer,
Joan Iaconetti

EARTH TONES

Earth colours are useful for depicting a large number of subjects, not only ones related to landscapes. They are ideal for mixing and combining. You can use them for less luminous areas of the painting, and they help create contrasts. The burnt earth tone is dark brown. Sienna earth has a subtle chocolate tone. Ochre is lighter and yellowy. Natural earth is a brown you can use to darken lighter tones.

Early autumn,
Hsin-I Kuo

66

DIFFERENT PAPER VARIETIES

Watercolour paper is available in different weights and textures. The best paper to choose will depend on the technique you are using and your personal preferences.

67

COLOURS THAT SHOULD NOT BE MIXED

The cadmiums with emerald green • Cobalt violet with the ochres. Ultramarine blue with emerald green. • Ultramarine blue with chrome yellow • Ultramarine blue with alizarin. • Vermilion with lead colours. • Cadmium red with viridian or Prussian blue.

68

HOW DO YOU MIX SKIN COLOUR WITH WATERCOLOURS?

Many artists find it challenging to mix colours to obtain a skin tone using watercolour paints. When working on a portrait or painting figures, they can be intimidated by how difficult it is to control watercolour paint and correct colours once they have been applied to the paper. Skin tones should contain a mixture of red, yellow and blue, adjusted while creating the painting, to realistically capture shadow, light and variations in skin tone. Palettes of skin colours will also vary depending on the skin tone and ethnic origin of the subject being painted.

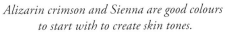

*Alizarin crimson and Sienna are good colours
to start with to create skin tones.*

THE COLOUR WHEEL

The term colour wheel refers to a circular graph comprising the six colours that are reflected when visible light from the solar spectrum is decomposed. It is based on the following order: purple, red, yellow, green, cyan blue, dark blue. Consequently, in principle, there would be three primary colours (purple, yellow and cyan blue), and three secondary colours (red, green and dark blue). These colours are completed by a further six, which result from mixing the primary colours with their nearest secondary colours. This leaves the colour wheel comprising twelve colours: three primary colours (P), three secondary colours (S) and three tertiary colours (T). It is important to underline that watercolours do not coincide exactly with the colours of light, which means each artist has to adapt their colour wheel.

70

PRIMARY COLOURS

These colours cannot be obtained by mixing any others, which means they are considered to be absolute and unique. They are yellow, cyan blue and magenta. It is important to note that cyan blue is unavailable in the artist's colour portfolio. This colour is available only in graphic art and photography. That is why what a painter considers to be the primary colours will normally not coincide with the primary colours used in colour theory. Various solutions are available to resolve this inconvenience. One would be to use a medium yellow, cerulean blue and alizarin carmine. However, when painting with watercolours, cerulean blue can appear opaque and dirty, which leads some painters to replace it with ultramarine blue or thalo blue. The yellow can be substituted by light cadmium yellow, and magenta by alizarin crimson.

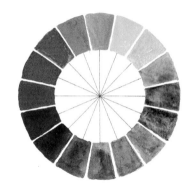

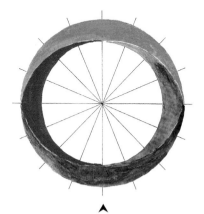

Colour wheel taken from the book Outlines of a Theory of the Light Sense, by **Ewald Hering** *(1878).*

◄ *Artists should try to avoid using pure colours in the background of their paintings.*

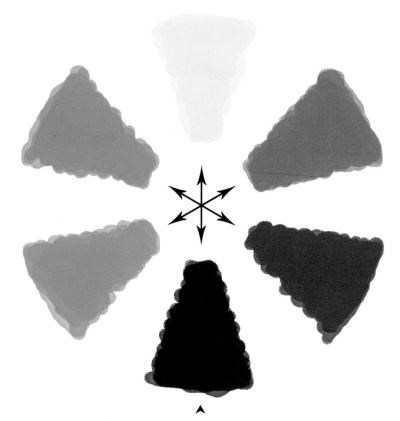

SECONDARY COLOURS

This refers to colours that are obtained by mixing two primary colours 50-50. That is how you obtain green (S), violet (S) and orange or red-orange (S). Starting with yellow and going clockwise, the first secondary colour you will find is green (the result of a mixture, in equal parts, of yellow and blue). By mixing these two colours (primary = yellow + secondary = green) you obtain the tertiary colour yellow-green (T). Moving along, the next primary colour (P) is blue, which, when mixed with yellow, forms the secondary colour green. When blue is mixed with green (primary = blue + secondary = green), the colour blue-green is created. The other secondary colour of blue, when it is mixed with red, is violet. When blue is mixed with violet (primary = blue + secondary = violet), you get violet-blue.

Diagram showing the secondary colours.

Because there are three primary colours, scientists will typically use a triangle to classify them. ▶

TERTIARY OR INTERMEDIARY COLOURS

The term tertiary or intermediary colour refers to colours obtained by mixing a primary and a secondary colour. In reality, they are no more than different colour hues. A tertiary colour is obtained by mixing a primary (P) and a secondary (S) colour in equal parts. They are yellow-green (T), blue-green (T) blue-violet (T), red-violet (T), red-orange (T) and yellow-orange (T). Tertiary colours are the most abundant in nature and so they are the most used in painting. Because of them, the most intense colours shine and colours with a medium intensity come to life.

PAPER THICKNESS

Unlike paper for drawing and etching, watercolour paper has a certain thickness, since this reduces paint absorption by the paper. The pigments are left on the surface of the paper, so the brilliance of the colours is preserved.

QUATERNARY COLOURS

These are the colours obtained by mixing tertiary colours with each other. Consequently, tertiary red + tertiary yellow = neutral orange; tertiary yellow + tertiary blue = very neutral green (olive green); and tertiary red + tertiary blue = neutral violet, similar to plum.

Taking the herd home, **Hsin-I Kuo** ➤

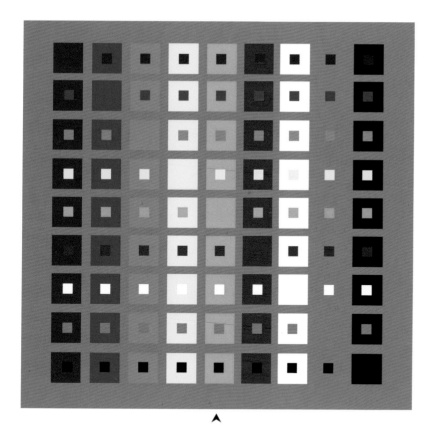

Table of different harmonious combinations.

COLOUR INTERACTIONS: HARMONY

Harmony means coordinating the different values that colours acquire in a composition. In other words, it is when all the colours in a composition have something in common with the rest of the colours that comprise it. In a harmonious combination, the artist may modulate the same tone or different tones. But, when mixing the paint, they use some of the same pigments as in the other colours.

Bottles on wooden box, **Laurin McCracken**

TONE CONTRAST

This occurs when the artist uses different colour tones.

LIGHT-DARK CONTRAST

The extreme point of this type of contrast is represented by black and white.

Pond with lotus and koi, **Hsin-I Kuo**

Underwood typewriter, **Laurin McCracken**

78

SATURATION CONTRAST

———

This is generated by modulating a pure saturated tone using white, black, grey or a complimentary colour.

79

THE TYPE OF PAPER TO USE

———

Watercolour paper can be quite expensive. While this may be the case, it is important to bear in mind that, if you want to get the best results, you have to use the best materials, if the work you are performing merits this. If, on the other hand, you are working on a sketch, practising, or if you are a beginner, you could choose cheaper paper. It is important to remember that paper for printing or drawing, thin card, cardboard and other types of paper and artistic surfaces are unsuitable for use with watercolours, since the result will not be what you expect.

QUANTITY CONTRAST

This is when the artist contrasts the large with the small, so no colour has any preponderance over another.

◄ *Fruit seller,*
Kwan Yuen Tam

 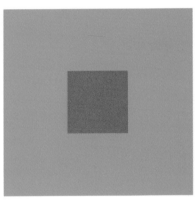 

▲
Combinations involving simultaneous contrast.

▲
Contrasting combinations between complementary colours.

SIMULTANEOUS CONTRAST

This is produced as a result of the influence each tone exercises on the others, and through juxtaposing them in a graphic composition.

CONTRAST BETWEEN COMPLEMENTARY COLOURS

To achieve a more harmonious result, it is best for one of the colours to be a pure colour, with the other being modulated using black or white. The pure tone should occupy a very limited surface area, since the extension of a colour in a composition should be inversely proportional to its intensity.

CONTRAST BETWEEN WARM AND COOL TONES

This is a contrast where some tones belong to the warm colour group, and others to the cool one.

An example of the result of combining warm and cool colours.

White block-out is a creative way of achieving extremely attractive results,
Líneke Zubieta

WHITE BLOCK-OUT

Using a clean, dry sheet of watercolour paper, the artist applies masking fluid, also called masking liquid, and leaves it until it is completely dry before painting over it. Depending on the artist's 'school', this technique can be used more formally or more creatively.

HOT-PRESSED PAPER

Hot-pressed paper has a smooth surface. It is the best choice when working with fine details, whether with watercolour paint, pencil or ink. It is also a good option when using watercolours as a base for colour pencils.

HOW TO APPLY MASKING FLUID

You can use masking fluid directly from the bottle or flask to create irregular shapes, but it can also be applied using a brush. When performing this task, it is a good idea to use an old paintbrush, since the composition of the masking fluid may damage it. If no old paintbrushes are available, you could use a new one, but it would be a good idea to protect it beforehand using petroleum jelly or, as explained earlier, to wash it thoroughly after use. This is a very important point since, due to its composition, block-out fluid is permanent once dry.

Apply masking fluid when producing your sketch. ▶

PICTORIAL SUBJECTS AND MASKING FLUID

This product is ideal if you want to paint straight, clear and precise profiles. It is good for defined shapes, like buildings, sails, grass, figures with white, or any shape you wish to contrast against the background. Artists will commonly use this liquid when they want a light colour to stand out on a dark background, as in nocturnal scenes, still lifes or similar subjects involving sharp, light-coloured profiles.

◄ *Iris,*
Chung-Wei Chien

APPLICATIONS FOR MASKING FLUID

The main function of masking fluid is to maintain the white of the paper. When the artist applies this product correctly, they can paint without worrying because the white of the paper will remain unaltered. This liquid is also used to outline parts of a painting or artwork—which can be useful for working zone by zone—, to achieve effects and highlights, and to produce negative paintings.

Different examples of masking fluid use.

HOW TO REMOVE MASKING FLUID

Once the masking has dried and you have finished your painting, it is time to remove the masking fluid. All you have to do is rub it with an eraser or your finger. You may also be able to peel it off, if the layer is thick enough. There is no need to worry about removing parts of your work that you want to keep because, as mentioned earlier, masking fluid has its own colour. This makes it easy to identify when the time comes to remove it from your artwork.

Permanente   Removible

Example of the difference between permanent and removable masking fluid.

90
COLD-PRESSED PAPER

Cold-pressed paper has a special texture, which may not be appropriate for work involving a lot of detail. Nevertheless, in other cases, it may be a highly versatile surface, and it is ideal for most watercolour techniques. Cold-pressed paper is the most popular paper type among beginners. There is no standard surface for cold-pressed paper.

Dry and wet techniques

This chapter discusses four basic techniques. They are the most important or most used. These techniques encompass watercolour painting on wet paper and dry paper, and variants of this.

MAKING YOUR OWN MASKING FLUID

As discussed earlier, masking fluid is a flexible adhesive applied to the paper before painting with watercolours. Once the paint is dry, the masking fluid can be removed using a soft eraser or your fingers, and this will reveal the white surface underneath it. While numerous brands offer masking fluid for artists to purchase, you can prepare you own formula using any latex-based adhesive. Rubber cement also works well as a masking fluid, particularly on canvas.

PERMANENT MASKING MEDIUM

Permanent masking medium is used to cover certain areas of paper and make them waterproof. This medium can also be mixed with watercolours, and it is ideal for isolating detailed areas. You should leave any sections you have treated using permanent masking medium to dry before you paint over them. A hair-dryer can be used to accelerate drying if necessary. Once dry, these areas are protected, and any subsequent layers cannot penetrate them.

HOW TO USE PERMANENT MASKING

You can apply permanent masking medium directly to the white paper or over dry layers of paint on the paper. You can also mix it with the watercolour paint first. While the layer of watercolour paint mixed with permanent masking medium remains wet, you can keep on manipulating it. Once dry, the area will become isolated.

In Moscow, **Chung-Wei Chien** ➤

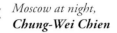
Moscow at night,
Chung-Wei Chien

94

PAINTING USING THE WET TECHNIQUE

'On wet' (also called 'in wet') is one of the most used watercolour techniques. To do it, the artist starts with wet paper. The technique involves the artist wetting or dampening the paper they are going to paint on, and then painting with the brush well charged with colour. If the artist wants to achieve a graded effect, for instance, they should use light, horizontal brush-strokes, while inclining the paper, so the colour runs. That is how the grading is achieved. It is also possible to achieve a completely flat colour, without any grading, simply by leaving the paper completely flat and charging the brush with the same amount of tint or colour for each brush-stroke. These layers of paint are called washes. Once the first layer is dry, different washes can be added on top of it. The artist should take special care with drying their watercolour. This is because, if previous washes are not completely dry, the colours can become mixed, which normally produces undesired effects.

Best friends,
Linda Doll

PAINTING USING THE WET-ON-WET TECHNIQUE

———

This technique is also called the 'wet paper' technique. That is because, to achieve the desired effect, you have to dampen the paper using the paintbrush and heavily dilute the colours with water. The technique in itself involves applying one colour on top of another, while the first colour is still wet. This causes the colours to fuse and disperse themselves in the direction of the line the artist has produced with the help of the water. Using this technique, the artist can allow free movement, or direct and guide it. The technique can be performed using a paint-brush, a pipette, by splattering the paint and using other tools. It is a good way to generate different effects in a landscape or in the background, for instance. This technique is ideal for softening the transition between different colours.

Morning run, **Linda Doll**

96

▼

PAINTING USING THE TECHNIQUE OF VARYING THE WASH THROUGH MINGLING

———

This technique has to be performed on a colour that is still wet. The purpose is to change or vary the original tone or colour in the places the artist requires. In other words, this is a type of wet-on-wet overlaying. It offers a wide range of possibilities for achieving difference effects in landscapes, architecture, skies and clothing, for instance.

HOW TO USE PERMANENT MASKING

You can apply permanent masking medium directly to the white paper or over dry layers of paint on the paper. You can also mix it with the watercolour paint first. While the layer of watercolour paint mixed with permanent masking medium remains wet, you can keep on manipulating it. Once dry, the area will become isolated.

PAINTING USING THE DRIP TECHNIQUE

The drip technique involves taking advantage of the moment when the paint is still wet to deposit one or several drips from a well-charged paintbrush on top of it. The brush may be charged with pure water, with the same colour at a different intensity, or with a different colour. The drip will casually mingle with the layer underneath, though the artist should always guide this, by inclining the paper to one side or the other, bearing in mind how wet it is at that moment.

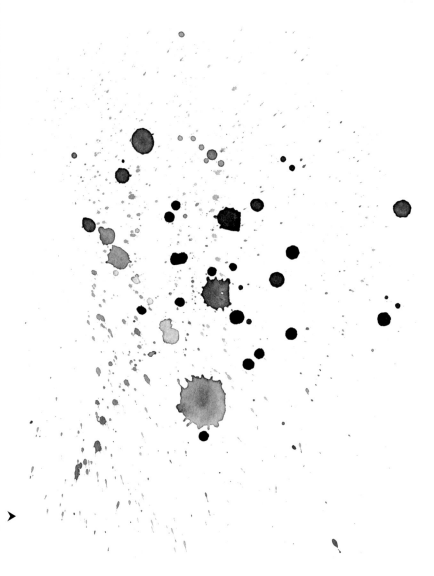

Detail showing what the paper looks like after using the drip technique. ➤

HOW TO MANAGE THE DRIP TECHNIQUE

Obviously, the artist will achieve different results if the paper is very wet and the brush they use to create the drip is charged with a small amount of pigment, compared to if the paper is fairly dry and the brush is well charged. In the first case, the colour will be diluted by the background colour. In the second, it will mingle with it, but the edges will remain well defined and radiant.

The drips slide over the paper.

MIXING COLOURS USING THE DRIP TECHNIQUE

When a colour is mixed with another using the drip technique, as long as the artist does not touch them afterwards, it will create a disintegrated, unbalanced composition, where the two colours, though mixed, can be observed separately. This is an ideal technique for skies, foliage and skin. It is also an excellent option for painting clouds. This is because dripping golden, warm colours with high transparency on illuminated parts, and cool and more intense colours on areas of shadow, can give life to different types of clouds.

This image shows a painting where the colours have been mixed using the drip technique.

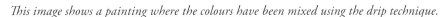

THE RESULT OF USING THE DRIP TECHNIQUE

Dripping paint can change any wash and produce richer qualities, with excellent textural effects. If you want to use the drip technique on a wash that is already dry, you have to dampen it using enough clean water to soften the previously applied colour. The right moment to apply drips of paint is when the wash is soft, without the paper being excessively saturated with water.

Detail of the drip technique,
Karin Johannesson

TRANSITIONS BETWEEN COLOURS

If you want to achieve gradual transition from one colour to another, without there being a clear division between them, this is the technique to use. After having deposited the first colour on the paper using sufficient water, brush on the second colour, while inclining the board approximately 15°. This way, the colours will mingle. Once you have achieved this mingling in your selected area, return the board to a horizontal position and continue adding the second colour. This will allow you to achieve attractive fusions, which will be useful and highly effective for skies, highlights, and landscapes.

This painting illustrates the effects of creating transitions between colours.

PAINTING USING THE DRY-ON-WET TECHNIQUE

———

This technique involves adding a dry colour on top of a wet base. The dry tone will blend into it, but not completely.

PAPER WEIGHT AND GRAMMAGE

———

The weight of paper is measured in grams. The more grams, the more the paper weighs and the thicker it will be. Watercolourists will normally use 300 g paper. This is because it works well for most of the artist's purposes. If you are planning to use a large quantity of paint or several washes, much heavier papers are available.

Day at the Beach, **Matej Jan**

PAINTING USING THE WET-ON-DRY TECHNIQUE

In the wet-on-dry technique, wet watercolour paint is applied to a dry surface. Once applied, the paint remains in place, without running, and the dry contours are well defined. In fact, it will blend only if the artist forces it to, by adding water along the edges. This is a good way of controlling the paint. In wet-on-dry watercolour painting, the artist applies various faint washes to the paper, overlaying one colour with another, but only once the layer underneath is dry. Using a dry brush, it is possible to add colours that are much more intense.

STEPS FOR PERFORMING THE WET-ON-DRY TECHNIQUE

It is important to remember to start by drawing a sketch using a pencil, to clearly define the layers of paint and start overlaying them. When overlaying colours, it is essential to remember that if you are going to combine warm colours directly on the paint, you must always apply the warmest colour first. For instance, if you want to obtain an orange, you should start by adding a red layer and, once it has dried, you should then add the yellow. With cool colours, the process works in reverse, and the first colour to add is the coolest one, followed by one that is less cool.

Visit, **Linda Doll** ➤

Under the bridge, **Ian Ramsay**

Farm near Panguitch, **Ian Ramsay**

KEY FEATURES OF THE WET-ON-DRY TECHNIQUE

Some of the best things about using the wet-on-dry technique is that it is easy to learn and very useful when you want to achieve greater precision in the details. To intensify a colour, all you have to do is apply a new layer over the preceding ones, once they are dry.

Spring in the mountains, **Irina Sztukowski**

108

PAINTING USING THE DRY-ON-DRY TECHNIQUE

The dry-on-dry technique refers to applying colour to watercolour paper that is completely dry, using a dry brush and pigment or paint that is virtually undiluted. Once the painted area has dried, or directly on the white of the paper, the artist creates lines or brushstrokes using the watercolour paint, but almost without dampening it, which will create a scratchy effect. This technique will allow the artist to overlay colours, while generating different transparencies where the colours overlap each other.

OVERLAYING COLOURS USING THE DRY TECHNIQUE

Applying a colour over another that has already dried, that is, overlaying, is an extremely important part of watercolour painting. It is considered a necessary process for adding abstract qualities to the colour. The basic, general or background colour will influence all transparent colours placed over it. Just as when you work with wet layers, when adding dry layers, apply the warmest colour first. If you do the reverse, and start by adding a cool colour, then place the warm one on top, the result will be completely different. This is because the cool colour neutralises the warm one, and dirties it.

Solitary enjoyment, **Hsin-I Kuo**

110

PAINTING USING THE DRYBRUSH TECHNIQUE

Working with a dry brush is one of the most difficult techniques to do well. You have to shake the container holding the paint very well, to make sure the mixture is homogeneous, before pouring a few drops onto your palette. Using a flat paintbrush, dip the bristles a quarter way into the paint. Discharge the brush onto a porous surface using very quick brush-strokes, until the brush-strokes stop leaving a mark.

*Spring, **Hsin-I Kuo***

PAINTING USING THE SEMI-DRY-BRUSH TECHNIQUE

The semi-dry-brush technique is the most common one. People often confuse it with the drybrush technique. The difference lies in how you apply the paint you have placed on the tip of your brush. With the semi-dry-brush technique, the area is emphasised much more quickly, which means, what would have been a mistake in the drybrush technique becomes the way to perform the semi-dry-brush technique. The artist will be able to make the area stand out with the first few brush-strokes. One of the main uses of the semi-dry-brush technique is when you have to paint large areas.

*Ilwaco Dock, **Ian Ramsay***

112

CHOOSING YOUR PAPER

Once you are familiar with the different types of paper available and their weight, you will have to decide what size and format will be most suitable. You will also have to choose between sketchbooks, pads, sheets and rolls.

113

PAINTING A UNIFORM BACKGROUND ON DRY PAPER USING A BRUSH

Use your paintbrush to directly apply colour onto dry paper. It is difficult to achieve a uniform background using this technique, and you have to do it very quickly. Generally speaking, you should not put the same amount of watercolour paint on every section.

PAINTING A UNIFORM BACKGROUND ON DRY PAPER USING A SPONGE

It is easier to achieve a uniform tone on dry paper using a sponge, since this will allow you to distribute the watercolour paint more evenly across the paper.

◄ *Little sun,* **Hsin-I Kuo**

This is an example of a background painted on dry paper using a sponge. ➤

115

PAINTING A UNIFORM BACKGROUND ON WET PAPER USING A BRUSH

This involves using the wet-on-wet technique. You dampen the paper beforehand and use the brush to distribute the colour across the wet surface.

116

PAINTING A UNIFORM BACKGROUND ON WET PAPER USING A SPONGE

Again, this involves using the wet-on-wet technique, but with a sponge instead of a paintbrush. The sponge allows you to spread the colour evenly over the surface.

A wet brush being used to paint on paper that has been previously dampened.

117

GRADING

Grading involves a transition in tone and/or colour. So, it may be monochromatic, or involve different colours.

Graded patches in different colours.

66

MONOCHROMATIC GRADING

―

This involves using the same colour, with different degrees of opacity, from darker to lighter, or vice versa.

◄ *The sky in this painting was produced using a sponge on wet paper,* **Carlos Martín**

This image shows a painting created by grading a single colour. ►

GRADING WITH DIFFERENT COLOURS

This involves making a transition from one colour to another.

 Example to show what it looks like when grading is applied to different colours.

120
PROTECTING YOUR PAINTBRUSHES

Avoid accumulating particles of pigment at the base of your brush. If this starts to happen, separate the hairs and prevent the accumulation from forming at the tip.

121
GRADING TECHNIQUES

It is possible to create grading using the same systems as for uniform backgrounds: wet-on-dry and wet-on-wet techniques. In the latter case, it is best to raise or incline your board a little, so the paint will run slightly. For a smoother appearance, you can pass a wet brush, without any pigment, over the paint, to spread it more effectively, particularly if you are using the wet-on-wet technique.

Landscape in the morning, **Hsin-I Kuo**

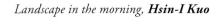

Autumn colours, **Hsin-I Kuo**

BACKGROUND GRADED FROM DARK TO LIGHT ON DRY PAPER USING A BRUSH

—

With this technique, the borders will be fairly uneven. Apply the colour with the brush well charged with pigment and a little water on the tip. Progressively dissolve and lighten it using water, while moving downwards.

BACKGROUND GRADED FROM DARK TO LIGHT ON WET PAPER USING A BRUSH

—

This involves the same process as described above, but you dampen the paper beforehand.

BACKGROUND GRADED FROM LIGHT TO DARK USING A BRUSH

—

When grading from light to dark, it is best to start in the middle of the paper, using the lightest tone. You have to start by dampening the upper section of the paper. Apply the lightest tone in the middle and spread it over the wet part. Grade the tone until it is at its lightest. Next, repeat the same process, but using a medium tone and starting at a lower part of the paper. So, you are grading from the darkest part.

Example of a painting where the artist dampened the paper before performing grading,
Tayete Garcia

BACKGROUND WITH OVERLAPPING COLOURS

To achieve this, you have to dampen half the paper beforehand. Apply the colour to the dry part and spread it over the wet. Leave it to dry and repeat the process using a different colour. You can repeat this process several times, depending on the number of colours you want to overlay.

Example of brush-strokes where the artist has performed grading from light to dark.

▲

Summer dream, **Hsin-I Kuo**

TECHNIQUES FOR PAINTING SKIES

Skies are always painted wet, with the artist using water to dampen the part of the paper the sky will occupy, and releasing a lot of colour. One good piece of advice is not to be afraid when applying colour to the sky.

Example of what a sky looks like in its initial phase. ▶

127

PAINTING SKIES

At one extreme, there is a clear sky, and at the other, a cloudy one. In the middle, there is an enormous number of possibilities.

128

CLEAR SKIES

If the sky is going to be completely clear, i.e. just blue, it would be best to use two or three tones of blue to vary its appearance, positioning the warmest blue tones at the highest parts.

Ferry, **Hsin-I Kuo**

129

CLOUDY SKIES

If your sky is going to have cumulus clouds, with a cotton-like appearance, you will have to paint them by lifting colour from the surface you have flooded with blues. You can do this by pressing down on it (without sideways movement) using a slightly damp piece of natural or artificial sponge, blotting paper or even cellulose toilet paper.

Evening at Saint Mark's Basilica, **Chung-Wei Chien**

Typical example of a clear sky,
Consuelo Córcoles

BRUSH CARE

Keep your brushes out of
direct sunlight.

Winter road,
Ian Ramsay ➤

TECHNIQUES

It is important to remember that there is no such thing as all possible techniques, since the only limit in this field is the artist's imagination. However, the artist should always keep the basic techniques in mind, like wet-on-wet, wet-on-dry, dry-on-wet and dry-on-dry.

ADDING COLOUR

This refers to adding paint to areas that are still wet. The control lies in dampening only the areas where the artist wants the colours to mingle.

GRADED LAYERS

This refers to a method for painting with watercolours that is closely related to the wet-on-wet technique. Here, there is just the right amount of dampness to allow the colours to fuse. These layers are used in areas that do not require definition or detail.

Example of a painting where the artist has used the technique of adding colour,
Tan Suz Chiang

MULTICOLOURED LAYERS

When an artist uses more than one colour, they create a multi-coloured layer. Landscape paintings will often begin with a multi-coloured layer, with blue or grey at the top. This is usually modified to yellow and green towards the foreground. Sunsets are another subject where multicoloured layers are typically used.

Blonde,
Matej Jan ➤

◄ *Saint Michael's church,*
Antonio Sánchez Serrano

OVERLAYING

—

Overlaying is a different way of referring to the wet-on-dry technique. In this case, the artist should leave each layer to dry before painting the next one. It is the ideal technique for creating texture and details in the foreground.

STORING YOUR BRUSHES

—

If you are going to store your brushes for a long time, make sure you clean and dry them thoroughly. Once you have made sure of this, store them in a sealed box.

Farm, **Ian Ramsay**

Dramafications, **Jean Gill**

BACK-RUNS

When you start painting with watercolours, you will make different mistakes, which will give rise to shapes that look like cauliflowers. What is interesting about these mistakes is that they can be used to create texture. If you paint one patch in a strong colour and, while it is still wet, apply a colour with a higher water content to it, the pigment will move away from the water, towards the edges. This is known as a back-run or water blossom. The basic idea is that if back-runs are created, it is because the artist did it deliberately. It can be a useful method for painting flowers.

138

GRANULATION

This is another way of taking advantage of mistakes. Some pigments, due to their mechanical specifications, are known as sedimentary colours. They tend to precipitate when mixed with water. The result is a textured surface, which is very useful when painting bark or stone façades.

Walk in the sun, **Chung-Wei Chien**

Covered bridge, **Ian Ramsay**

139

GRADING

This is the smooth transition from one colour or tone to another. Each movement should be lighter in tone than the preceding one. The artist applies a charged brush to the lower edge of the patch. It is a good idea to always move the brush in the same direction and not go over the same place twice. Wet-on-wet is the most usual way to achieve grading, although there are other ways of doing it. It is used a lot for clouds.

140

BLEEDS

Bleeds may appear when the artist applies a layer on top of another that is not completely dry. It is possible to control bleeds with the paper. The more absorbent the paper is, the more difficult it will be to create a bleed. Bleeding can generate texture, for instance, highlights in calm water. You can correct a bleed by applying water and starting again.

An example of bleeding. ➤

BRUSH DRAWING

This is considered an art among Chinese and Japanese watercolour painters. In the West, it refers to traditional drawing using a paintbrush. It is essential to use a hard paintbrush. Depending on the pressure you apply to the brush, you can create everything from lines to a print of the brush. This technique is used to create movement.

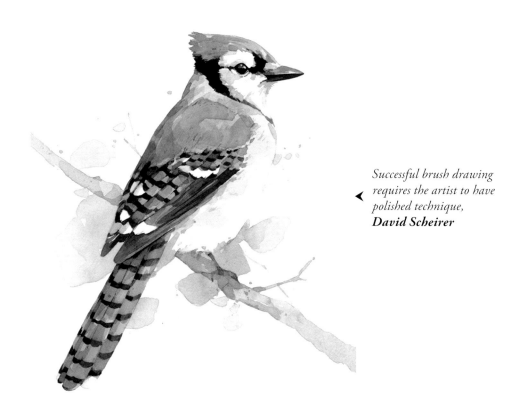

Successful brush drawing requires the artist to have polished technique, **David Scheirer**

STAINING

This is performed with liquid watercolours. Stains are difficult to control, with fate playing a role, but they produce different visual forms, which can be useful for starting a subject. The factors involved in creating a stain include the height from which a drip falls, steadiness of hand, paper inclination, the extent to which the drip is absorbed and how wet the paper is. They can be used to add texture to trees and small stones.

▲

Erguvanlar, **Ayşe Eylül Sönmez**

▲

Istanbul, **Ayşe Eylül Sönmez**

OTHER RECOMMENDATIONS FOR LOOKING AFTER YOUR BRUSHES

It is a good idea to use moth repellent when you store your brushes. But even if you do, remember it is not a completely trustworthy way of preventing damage caused by moths.

Backgrounds, **Jean Gill**

COMBINED METHODS

This refers to artworks that use more than one technique. In fact, most paintings will be combined works. You can create a watercolour using only wet-on-wet, which will, generally speaking, produce a bland and/or blurry artwork. When working on details and definition, it is better to use the wet-on-dry technique.

MIXING ON THE PAPER

Watercolourists will normally mix their colours on the palette. But, you can achieve more subtle effects, if you mix the tones, or if you continue mixing them, on the paper.

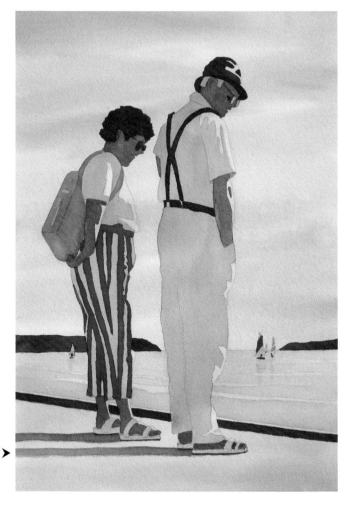

Day trip, **Linda Doll** ➤

Oyambre marshes, **Francisco Peral Bárcena**

Journey towards life, **Tan Suz Chiang**

DIRECTED BRUSH-STROKES

——

This involves using brush-strokes to evoke something real. For instance, foliage being blown by the wind can be depicted using long brush-strokes in a specific direction. This will convey the required feeling of movement and dynamism.

NEGATIVE SPACE

——

Negative space is used to achieve a high level of luminance. It is best to use the paper itself, by leaving it blank. This involves planning your artwork in advance, to know which parts of the paper you have to leave dry, before applying paint around them.

MASKING FLUID

——

Masking fluid should be applied to dry paper. You have to let it dry completely before painting over it. It is used to maintain the white of the paper, to enable the artist to paint freely, without destroying the white. The colour of the masking fluid will help you identify it, so you can easily remove it at the end. The most common applications of this technique are when the artist produces their painting part by part, when they want to include highlights and when creating negative space. Since masking fluid is permanent once it is dry, it is best to use an old paintbrush to apply it. Another option is to cover the brush in petroleum jelly before dipping it in the masking fluid.

Moscow after rain,
Chung-Wei Chien ▶

HIGHLIGHTING BY LIFTING

When you want to achieve gentle highlights, it is more effective to lift the paint than to leave the paper blank or use masking fluid. If you want to perform this technique, use a slightly moistened brush at the end of the process.

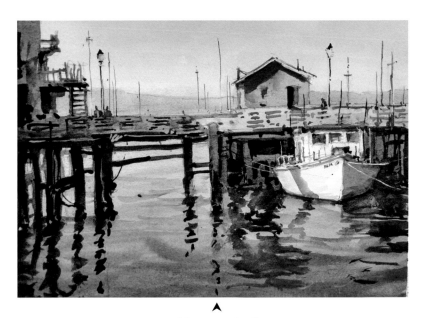

Monterey wharf,
Brienne M. Brown

MORE ON
BRUSH CARE

—

Wash the head of the brush in a jar of clean water.

LIFTING THE PAINT

—

The main reason for using this technique is to correct mistakes. However, it is sometimes used in combination with a wash, to create highlights, blur edges and produce movement. The key to controlling this technique resides in the paper and the colour you are lifting. To do it, you can use a sponge, paintbrush, cotton wool bud or masking fluid. To produce straight lines, use absorbent paper folded to the desired thickness.

▲

Venice at dusk,
Chung-Wei Chien

152

˅

DRYBRUSH TECHNIQUE

———

This technique is all about detail. The artist uses very little water on the brush and applies the colour with the paintbrush almost dry. This method offers a greater level of control, which means it is useful for creating texture and detail. Conversely, it is unsuitable for large areas, such as the sky or background.

▲

Feeding happily, **Hsin-I Kuo**

SPLATTERING USING A TOOTHBRUSH

Immerse the toothbrush in paint. Graze the bristles with your thumb to splatter the colour.

◄ *Painting in which splattering has been used,* **Tito Fornasiero**

SPLATTERING USING A SPRAY BOTTLE

You can do this with paint or water. Splattering can be used to lift colour, or you can add colour to the water in the bottle. The paint will follow the shape of the drips on the paper.

∧

Example of the textures an artist can achieve by playing with splattering.

SPRAYING

Using this technique, you can give life to textures and achieve a powerful effect. To produce it, you have to use a toothbrush or short hard-haired brush. Charge the brush with a fairly diluted colour and give it a few sharp taps, to create random patches. Next, charge the brush with another colour and less water and rake the bristles, to create new patches on top of the first ones, with the new patches being smaller. You can use this technique as many times as you want, until you obtain the result you are looking for.

En example of spraying.

SCRAPING

While the paint is still wet, you can scrape it using a hard-haired brush, to lift it or lighten the colours. You can also use this technique to add highlights. Once the paint is dry, with the help of a razor or credit card, make an energetic movement over certain areas—particularly effective on grainy papers—to remove the colour from the most salient parts of the paper, creating interesting effects of light and texture.

Night in Venice, **Chung-Wei Chien**

157

**PROTECTING
YOUR BRUSHES**

Remove any excess water
that may have been left
among the bristles by shak-
ing the brush vigorously
with small, sharp wrist
movements.

Monologue, **Hsin-I Kuo**

158

CRYSTAL OR SNOW EFFECT

To create a crystalline effect on water or portray snow on a landscape, you can use salt. You should use the salt while the colours are still wet on the paper. You have to calculate the moment when you are going to add the grains of salt, to ensure there is sufficient dampness, though the paper should not be excessively wet. To achieve other similar effects, you can use polystyrene balls in the same way as salt. Another variant is to use thread while the colours are still wet and then let them dry. Once your watercolour is dry, remove what is left of the salt, balls or thread.

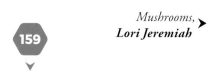

Mushrooms, ➤
Lori Jeremiah

159

CARDBOARD STAMPING

One way of achieving straight
lines is to use thick cardboard that
is as rigid as possible. The idea is
to coat one of its edges. This edge
is the one you will subsequently
stamp on the paper.

PAINTING WITH AN ATOMISER

Though infrequent, some water-colour artists use atomisers to achieve certain effects in the sky and soil. Use a damp sponge to wet the area of sky you want to paint. Next, spray some of the borders of that area using an atomiser. When you add the colour, you will obtain interesting edges that you can achieve only by using an atomiser.

Image showing textures produced using an atomiser.

Floral motifs produced using a dry brush and excess water, ▶
Líneke Zubieta

161

EXCESS COLOUR AROUND THE EDGES

Sometimes, on certain layers, you may notice you have too much water. When this happens, it can generate a deposit of excess colour around the edges, creating hard, inconvenient borders. You can correct this problem while the paper is damp by using a dry or semi-dry brush to lift and reduce this excess. You can also reduce the surplus water using a sponge, clean cloth or blotting paper.

FLAT WASHES

The foundation of pure watercolour painting is the wash. This refers to applying colour over a large area, as if to cover it with a single brush-stroke. When performing this task, it is a good idea to start by dampening the area you are going to paint, selecting a large brush, in good condition, and mixing more paint than you need. If any edges of the wash are going to be tricky, then position the paper so the wash starts there. This may mean placing your sketch on its side or upside down. The first brush-strokes should follow the complicated part of the sketch, to ensure you create an even and transparent wash.

Example of flat and graded washes in the same painting,
Tayete Garcia

GRADED WASHES

This is similar to performing a flat wash. The difference in this case is that the colour will become progressively darker.

A PRACTICAL TIP ON BRUSHES

Carefully smooth the bristles between your thumb and forefinger to make sure all the hairs are in place.

VARIEGATED WASHES

These involve several colours. The artist applies different colours to wet paper, one after the other. They then allow them to mingle with each other, and find their own forms, in the area to be covered. You have to leave them alone and refrain from correcting or manipulating them until they are dry. Only then, if you wish, should you make additions or deletions.

Variegated washes in the same colour, but with different tones,
Karin Johannesson

91

Bird, **Hsin-I Kuo**

166

DOTTING

This task involves applying dots of colour onto the surface of the paper. This technique is normally used to portray textures, in which case, it can be applied over washes.

167

SCRUBBING

This involves applying the pigment to the paper with a rubbing movement, so the paper is covered in different directions. This can be useful to bring out the texture of the paper.

◄ *The Tuscan sun,* **Chung-Wei Chien**

168

LINE-AND-WASH TECHNIQUE

Lines are useful for adding fine details and dark tones where necessary. The line-and-wash technique is very different. The artist uses lines to draw the entire scene or figure. They then apply washes to extend or unify the picture. Sometimes they will apply the washes over the lines, but they will also use lines to define the washes, by accentuating forms and reinforcing the drawing. Numerous artists produce monochrome line-and-wash sketches. However, you can obtain excellent results by using coloured washes and black lines, or even black washes and coloured lines.

169

SPONGE ON DRY PAPER

You can use a sponge to produce interesting textures on dry paper using a single colour, without diluting it too much.

170

MORE TIPS ON LOOKING AFTER YOUR BRUSHES

After smoothing down the bristles of the brush, you will have to clean the colour off your fingers. Some pigments, like alizarin, are resistant to rinsing. If your fingers are dirty after the cleaning process, that means the brush is dirty too.

Exit only, **Joan Iaconetti**

Harvest, **Hsin-I Kuo**

Gölyazı, **Ayşe Eylül Sönmez**

171

SPONGE STAMPING

If you successively use the sponge as if it were a stamp, applying two or three colours, you will be able to portray scrubland very effectively.

172

SPONGE ON WET PAPER

It is also possible to use a sponge on wet paper, to lift or lighten certain sections.

You can use a sponge to lighten certain areas,
Tan Suz Chiang

USING THE SPONGE TO REMOVE WASHES

Take a completely clean sponge and submerge it in water. Next, squeeze out half of the water and apply the sponge to the paint you want to remove. If, the first time you do this, the wash is not removed or reduced enough, repeat the process until it is completely eliminated, or until the tone is sufficiently lightened.

Ardagger, **Colin Maxwell**

SPONGE WITH PAINT ON PAPER

Another technique involving a sponge is to charge it with paint and apply it to the paper. This produces a mottled effect, where the paint and white paper are interspersed.

After the rain, **Chung-Wei Chien**

Bloom,
Hsin-I Kuo

WORKING WITH AN ERASER

You can use an eraser to reduce the intensity of a wash or an area that is too dark. To do this, the paint must be dry and the eraser clean.

Cambridge rider, ▶
Chung-Wei Chien

96

CLEANING YOUR BRUSH WITH SOAP

If you struggle to get your brush clean, you could use artist's (or standard) soap to clean it. To do this, wet the brush and apply the soap to the bristles. Rub it in the palm of your hand to create foam. Make sure the soap reaches right to the heel, at the end of the ferrule, and rinse under running water.

RAZORS

Razors can be used to scratch in such a way as to produce white lines and patches on the dry paint.

Deep stairs, **Joan Iaconetti**

ADDING WHITE PAINT TO WATER

Doing this changes the appearance of the paint. It can be appropriate for certain subjects.

ADDING GUM ARABIC TO THE PAINT

Scratching wet paint that has been treated with gum arabic will generate other effects, which may be desirable for your work. The result of using gum arabic is that the colours separate quickly, letting the razor slide through them and revealing the white paper underneath.

▲
Leaving spaces where the white paper is visible is a good technique for creating highlights in your painting,
Tito Fornasiero

180
⌄

USING SOAP

Adding soap to your paint is a trick that will allow you to paint on surfaces that would not normally allow this, such as leaves, flowers and glass. Once the surface is dry, go over it again using fairly dry paint. If you then apply pressure on the other side, you can transfer the image to your paper or board.

Adding different elements to your watercolour technique is a good way of fostering creativity.

181

COTTON AND SAND TECHNIQUES

Adding these elements to your paint can create strange effects. It is worth experimenting with them.

DRYING YOUR BRUSHES

To dry your brushes, lay them flat on absorbent paper or an old towel. Once dry, keep them in a brush jar, with the bristles pointing upwards.

OFFSET PRINTING TECHNIQUE

This involves painting on a waterproof surface, like glass, plastic, a carton or waterproof paper, and then applying it to the paper by pushing down on the back of this surface. Another alternative is to randomly apply paint to a surface and then transfer it by applying a certain amount of pressure. You can transform the patches of paint by adding marks, washes, lines or dots, for instance.

Port of Nice, **Colin Maxwell**

184

BLOW PAINTING

Blowing hard from above on very wet drips can create branches that snake off in all directions. Afterwards, you can refine these accidental images.

Parts of this painting were produced using the blow-painting technique,
Guilhem Sals

185

WATERCOLOUR PENCILS

Watercolour pencils are colour pencils that, when mixed with water, allow the artist to imitate the watercolour technique, but using a much faster, simpler and safer process.

Bright over me, **Robyn Pees**

101

Example of a painting created with watercolour pencils, using the wet and dry techniques, **Domantas Didžiapetris** ▶

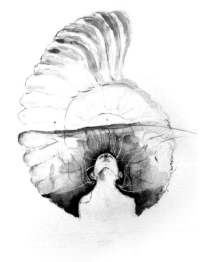

WATERCOLOUR-PENCIL TECHNIQUE

You can use these pencils dry or wet. The dry technique involves drawing your illustration using the colour pencils, and then stopping at that stage, without dampening the drawing. As an alternative, with the wet technique, you subsequently dampen the drawing, to create the effect of watercolour paint.

▲
The boot house, **Isabel Mancebo Balda**

HOW TO USE WATERCOLOUR PENCILS

When an artist wants to create a drawing, they will normally use permanent colour pencils. While this may be the usual technique, it is not the only option. In fact, one of various alternatives is to use watercolour pencils.

188

WATERCOLOUR-EFFECT TECHNIQUE

If you are producing a sketch, draw it dry and then pass a paint-brush dipped in water over it, to achieve the watercolour effect.

189

PREPARING A COLOUR IN THREE STEPS

1) Choose the colour that is most similar to the one you want to imitate or prepare.

2) Mix this tone with its complimentary tone until you find your desired intensity.

3) Lighten the colour, if necessary, until you achieve your desired value.

Christina Papagianni

Underwater intimacies, **Christina Papagianni**

190

DIRECT-EFFECT TECHNIQUE

———

If you pass a paintbrush dipped in water over the tip of the watercolour pencil, you will charge the hair of the paintbrush with colour. This way, you can use the paintbrush to paint directly onto the surface.

191

SANDING

———

Rub the tip of the watercolour pencil using fine-grain sandpaper. You can use the powder it creates to dust the parts of the artwork you want to colour. Afterwards, use a wet paintbrush to dissolve this dust.

192

MIXED-SANDING

———

This is a repetition of the preceding technique, but the artist uses several colours, to achieve a wider colour range.

Aracena Castle, **Luis Lomelino**

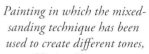

Landscapes are ideal for playing
with different colours,
Antonio Sánchez Serrano
⌄

Painting in which the mixed-
sanding technique has been
used to create different tones,
Vinita Pappas

Gouache

Gouaches are traditionally created using watercolour paint. India ink is another option, though this product may not be very pliant. It can lead to discontinuities and stains in the final work. In the following pages, you will find all the guidelines you need to manage this technique, which has so much in common with watercolour painting.

GOUACHE DEFINED

Watercolour and gouache painting both use paint dissolved in water, with the addition of a binder (principally made of gum arabic). One of the major differences between gouache and watercolour is that the paint used in gouache is more viscous and pasty.

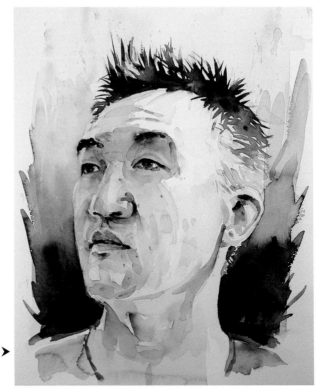

Face study, ➤
David Lobenberg

WHITE IN GOUACHE

Another difference is that, in gouache painting, white and light are not produced through the transparency of the paint on the paper, but instead, by using the colour white. The gouache technique allows the artist to use a wide range of colours, starting with a single base colour, which they develop through blending.

In this beautiful painting, you can appreciate the different tones of the colour palette from white to black, ➤
Tayete García

APPLYING GOUACHE

Gouache is normally applied using a brush. The difficulty—and the beauty—of this technique lies in knowing how to dilute the paint correctly, and capture the range from direct light to total shadow in your painting.

196

COLOUR

Any given colour is relative, since it is always influenced by the other colours that surround it.

The unvarnished truth of the matter,
David Lobenberg

197

PRODUCING A GOUACHE

Gouaches are traditionally created using watercolour paint. India ink is another option, though this product may not be very pliant. It can lead to discontinuities and stains in the final work. A good suggestion is to paint from lightest to darkest, since the layers build up over one another. The same paper is normally used for gouache as for watercolours. This means you have to use paper that is thick enough not to warp.

Multicoloured fish, **David Lobenberg**

FITTING FORMS TOGETHER WITH GOUACHE

Gouache is based on a completely transparent background. The value of the paint should always go from less to more, which means lighter tones should always be allowed to move towards darker ones. This is because lighter tones will permit tonal additions, and not vice versa. Consequently, from the outset, it is vital to establish the position of the main working areas in the drawing. This is the only way to determine exactly which tones will correspond to each area.

Example of how to fit forms together, with the background as the main focus,
Guilhem Sals

MODELS AND GOUACHE

The artist should analyse the model they are going to use for their artwork from a completely synthetic perspective. This means they should refrain from making any type of tonal assessment. One way of doing this is to use a pencil with the same tone as the gouache you are going to produce, and fit each of the forms together accurately.

Woman sitting on chair, **Charles Reid**

200

HOW TO CHANGE THE BACKGROUND IN GOUACHE PAINTING

Gouache painting always begins with lighter tones, which can be darkened as the drawing progresses. It is not possible to do this in reverse. So, you cannot paint a light tone over a dark base.

Morning light in Venice,
Ronald Hazell ▶

Road to Aldea de Portillo,
Tayete Garcia
▼

201

DIP PENS AND GOUACHE

Any dip pen work on a gouache painting should be performed once the gouache is completely dry. Otherwise, the ink from the pen will bleed into the entire wet area.

202

COLOUR IN OVERLAYS

When overlaying, the warmest colour should be applied first.

203

HOW TO PAINT A GOUACHE

The key to good gouache technique lies in a sound estimate of the distribution of light in the drawing. You can capture this by using more- or less-diluted gouache paint.

204

PAINTING A GOOD GOUACHE IN PRACTICE

Because there is a wide range of tones, your success will depend on assessing, and carefully comparing, the nuances you observe in the subject and throughout the rest of the drawing. It is therefore always best to proceed prudently. That is, it is best to increase the tonal intensity of any given part only after careful reflection.

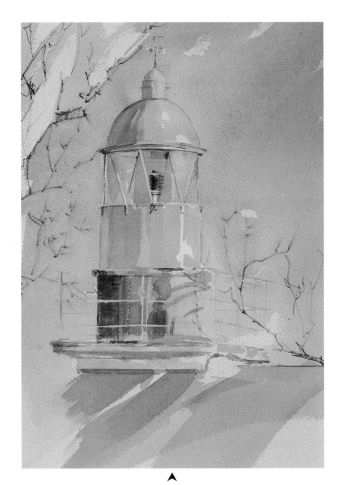

▲

La Cerda lighthouse, **Líneke Zubieta**

▲

Tétouan, **Luis Lomelino**

111

205

THE MOST APPROPRIATE COLOURS FOR A GOUACHE

All hues of brown, walnut, bistre, indigo, kaolin green, neutral tint, sanguine and carbon black are suitable for painting a gouache, as are brown watercolour paint, the different gouache colours and Sienna earth. Gouache can be applied without problems to pencil and ink drawings, and with caution to pastels, chalk and charcoal.

Painting produced in tones that are typical of gouache, ➤
Pauline Adair

Landscape, **Eduardo Marticorena**
∨

206

THE GOUACHE TECHNIQUE

Gouache is a cumulative technique. The artist starts by applying pale, transparent layers, and then adds layer upon layer, until they achieve the darkest tones. It is difficult to reduce the intensity of a tone that has already been applied to the drawing, so you should always avoid using too much paint. By applying successive layers that grow gradually darker—though they should always be transparent—, you will achieve the effect of velvety shadows. The procedure requires a lot of patience because you have to wait for each layer to dry before applying the next one.

HOW TO PREPARE THE PAPER FOR GOUACHE PAINT

Nowadays, the market offers hundreds of excellent papers for working with gouache. It is best to use watercolour paper. However, it is a good idea to experiment with papers of all kinds. That is the only way to discover the most suitable option for each case.

Mediterranean Light, **Antonio Sánchez Serrano**

208

ACHIEVING COLOUR LUMINANCE

Luminance is obtained when the artist applies well-mixed washes with a few brush-strokes, in the simplest way.

FLAT GOUACHE ON WET PAPER

In this technique, the first step is to wet the watercolour paper. Do this using a 4 or 5 cm flat brush. With another, smaller brush, add brush-strokes of paint diluted in water. Because the paper is wet, the water will spread easily. These washes can be used to create a graded background, for instance.

In this painting, the wet-on-wet technique can be very clearly seen, **Ayşe Eylül Sönmez**

WET-ON-WET GOUACHE TECHNIQUE

To create a gouache, moisten the paper with a brush before you start adding areas of colour.

Dusk on Gran Via, **Carlos Martín**

WET-ON-DRY GOUACHE TECHNIQUE

This technique is used when the paint is dry. The artist moistens it again with a brush, or applies more paint. It is useful for softening a profile that is already dry. To do this, dip the brush in clean water and pass it over the area. Release water from the brush and then mop it up again. The water will remove the previously dry colour.

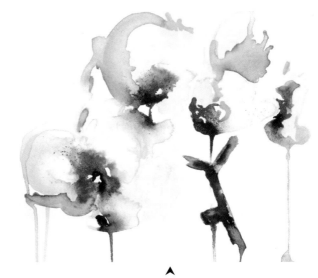

Drips running down the paper. This is achieved using the wet-on-dry technique,
Karin Johannesson

212

HOW TO FRAME A GOUACHE

This refers to the natural framing formed by the paper around the gouache, so, around the paint itself. To achieve framing of this type, you have to place special paper tape over the area you want to protect. Press it down firmly to make sure it sticks properly, so no paint can seep underneath it.

Beautiful painting with clear, contrasting profiles,
Colin Maxwell

213

FLAT GOUACHE

To create a flat gouache, put clean water in a well. Add paint, until you achieve the intensity you are looking for. Keep in mind that watercolour paint loses intensity when it dries. So, it looks more faded than when it is wet. It is a good idea to prepare a generous quantity of paint, to avoid it running out in the middle of your wash. Apply the paint with brush-strokes that go from side to side, like a pendulum.

214

CARLOS DE HAES

Carlos de Haes, a master of painting, always recommended that his students squint their eyes to see their work without the details. This way, they could appreciate all the parts of the painting at the same time.

Woman, ***Dámaso Carrillo***

Grading on the bird's feathers, **David Scheirer** ➤

215

⌄

GRADED GOUACHE

———

Start the gouache with the most saturated colour and progressively charge the brush with an increasing amount of clean water.

216

⌄

VARIEGATED GOUACHE

———

Blend several colours by subtly going from one to the next.

Several colours are blended across this painting, **Sylvie Guillot** ⌄

117

GOUACHE AND THE SPONGE EFFECT

Apply the watercolours with a sponge.

◄ *Gran Vía,* **Javier Fuentes**

GOUACHE AND SPLATTERING

Create splatters using a tooth-brush (or an old, blunted paint-brush). Lift off excess paint with a clean cloth.

◄ *Painting partly produced using the splattering technique,* **Francisco Peral Bárcena**

GOUACHE AND THE SALT EFFECT

Apply salt on top of the wet watercolour paint. It will absorb the water, creating a mottled appearance. Remove the salt only once the painting is completely dry.

Lavender fields, **Marene Lasagabaster**

220

A GENERAL TIP ON COLOUR

As a general rule, note that all colours, as they get further away, tend to melt into a neutral grey.

221

GOUACHE PAINTING WITH INK

Gouache is a wet technique that involves drawing with a paintbrush. One way to produce a gouache is to use India ink diluted in water. A grey gouache can be produced using black India ink, and a coloured gouache would result from using inks in a range of tones. Different intensities and a variety of hues can be achieved by diluting the ink with more or less water.

◄ *Chain smoking,* **Consuelo Córcoles**

WATERPROOF GOUACHE INK

This is one of the best inks for drawing because of its density. This ink is available in black and white, and you can also get 18 bright, transparent colours. The colours have lower photostability than black and white. Once the product is dry, it takes on a glossy appearance.

NON-WATERPROOF GOUACHE INK

You can buy special inks for drawing. They come in different colours and are similar to diluted watercolours. They penetrate the paper to a greater extent than drawing inks, are easy to dilute, and dry with a matte finish.

Castle Hardegg, **Colin Maxwell**

GOUACHE WASH

This refers to a tone or hue applied as a thin transparent layer. It can be applied through sweeping, wide brush-strokes, or with small, light touches. The subtle interplay of the gouache you produce will lie in creating darker and lighter contrasts. To lighten part of a colour, before it has dried, use a clean, dry paintbrush, sponge or cloth, to absorb the quantity you want to remove.

Water, **Javier Fuentes**

The morning walk, **Vinita Pappas**

**DARKENING
A COLOUR**

To darken a colour, never add black because this will change the colour. Instead, add a similar colour, following the order of the colour wheel. So, to darken a light yellow, add dark yellow, orange or red, but never black.

121

Watercolours by subject

There are infinite options when painting with watercolours. That is why this section focuses on some of the most typical subjects and gives advice on how to capture them.

Landscapes

STARTING TO PAINT LANDSCAPES

Before you start painting your landscape, it is a good idea to test your paints on a medium that will not be the final painting. That way, you will get a more finished idea of the form they will eventually take.

Infinite colours and tones can be used in landscapes. You might say that it is one of the subjects where it is easiest to choose your palette,
Brienne M. Brown

LANDSCAPES AS A RECOMMENDED SUBJECT

Landscapes are one of the best subjects for those starting out in the world of watercolour painting. This is because they are fairly simple. The main reason for their simplicity is that the forms they contain tend to be imprecise and do not require too much accuracy.

Morning stroll to the patch, **Brienne M. Brown**

The largest elements, like mountains, should be the priority in any landscape painting, **Brienne M. Brown**

STARTING TO SKETCH A LANDSCAPE

It is best to start at the horizon. From there, sketch the largest elements, like mountains, rocks, trees and plants. The next step is to paint the sky. To do this, use dark blue at the highest point of the painting and then grade the colour, to achieve the lightest blue at the point nearest the horizon.

COLOUR IN LANDSCAPES

If the landscape is going to have overlapping colours, apply the warmest one first. Then continue successively, following this premise.

SHADOWS IN THE LANDSCAPE

If you want to darken part of the landscape, do not apply black. Add a darker tone from within the colour wheel, to create the shadow. This way, you should be able to balance luminosity without too many problems.

A painting predominated by warm colours, **Consuelo Córcoles**

REFLECTIONS IN THE LANDSCAPE

Landscapes often require the artist to depict highlights or transparencies. This may occur when you have to paint glass or a reflection on water, for instance. To effectively portray a reflection, it is best to use a range of greys or whites, particularly if you want to depict the presence of a transparent element.

WATER IN THE LANDSCAPE

If your landscape is going to have a lake or reflections in the water, remember that the blue tone will have an effect on anything you have positioned behind it. So, for instance, if there is a yellow element in the background, then you should change it to a light green tone.

Weirs on Manzanares river, **Javier Fuentes**

FIGURES IN THE LANDSCAPE

When painting a landscape, visual perception is one of the points where you should take the greatest care. Figures in the background should not have strong hues or attention-grabbing colours. While you may want to highlight elements like mountains, it will work best to blur or grade them, as appropriate.

Going home, **Tito Fornasiero**

THE FOCAL POINT IN THE LANDSCAPE

All landscapes should have a feature of interest or focal point. If all the objects that comprise the landscape have the same importance, the resulting artwork will be overloaded or confusing. To avoid this happening, you have to choose a specific area or element in the painting that will dominate the rest and capture the onlooker's attention. Your painting could also contain two or three secondary elements that support the primary one.

Spaulding meadows,
Vinita Pappas

235

COMPOSITION IN A LANDSCAPE

The rules of composition will help you create a harmonious landscape. This is because everything in nature obeys certain geometric or mathematical patterns. This premise forms the basis for the different rules of composition.

Painting where the composition and mixture of colours create a harmonious work,
Javier Fuentes

Painting based on an unusual composition and palette,
Luis Lomelino

236

HOW TO APPLY COMPOSITION IN YOUR LANDSCAPE

There are several rules of composition that have been used since antiquity, such as the golden ratio (divine proportion or golden proportion), the golden spiral, and the rule of thirds. Besides being used in painting, they are also employed in architecture and other arts. However, to apply them, you have to perform certain mathematical operations. Some of these are very simple, while others are more complex.

THE RULE OF THIRDS IN LANDSCAPES

The rule of thirds involves dividing the image using two horizontal lines and two vertical ones, to create a division of nine equal parts. When you make this division, you can position the points of interest at the intersection of some of these horizontal and vertical lines. The result of using this trick is balance. This way, you will achieve a more harmonious composition.

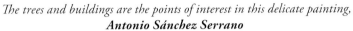

The trees and buildings are the points of interest in this delicate painting,
Antonio Sánchez Serrano

VISUALISING THE RULE OF THIRDS IN LANDSCAPES

On some cameras, including on mobile phones, you can select the option to show a grid based on the rule of thirds. This will help you take interesting photographs for painting landscapes, and achieve better composition in your artwork. Additionally, some graphic-design programs, like Photoshop, will let you crop an image while applying the rule of thirds, among other options.

Linares de la Sierra,
Luis Lomelino

Landscape, **Manuel Gandullo**

THE GOLDEN RATIO IN LANDSCAPES

This is a formula that different civilisations have used to inspire their artwork. It governs certain patterns in nature. The golden ratio involves a pattern based on a rectangle. While this rectangle can stand alone with defined limits, it can also be repeated infinitely, based on specific proportions.

240

GREEN IN LANDSCAPES

Green is a predominant colour in landscapes. If you want to make it less intense, add a little red. With a very small amount of red, you can control the colour without affecting quality too much. But, be careful, because the more red you add, the more earthy the colours will become.

Returning to barracks, **Ron Hazell**

PREPARING DIFFERENT GREEN TONES FOR A LANDSCAPE

If you need to lighten a green, to depict lighter parts in the foliage of a tree or a pasture, for instance, you may not be able to achieve this using only white. It may also be necessary to add yellow, if you want to preserve the warmness of the colour.

Light colours for a summertime landscape,
Francisco Peral Bárcena

PREPARING DIFFERENT GREEN TONES FOR A LANDSCAPE (2)

To make a green darker, you can add burnt Sienna or burnt umber, which will maintain the warmness. You could also use complimentary reds, which are usually dark reds.

River Mandeo,
Manuel Gandullo

A normal afternoon,
Antonio Sánchez Serrano

244

FINDING HARMONY IN LANDSCAPES

Using the blue in the sky to create the greens can help you achieve greater harmony in your painting.

243

THE DARKEST GREEN IN A LANDSCAPE

If you want a darker, but cool green, which can be well suited to some shadows, it is a good idea to darken it using a dark blue. In the darkest areas, add burnt umber and/or black.

245

VISUALISING THE COLOURS IN A LANDSCAPE

Look for different photographs of landscapes. This will help you see what the greens are like (besides containing yellows and blues) on a sunny day, a cloudy day, in the morning, in the afternoon, in the evening and during the different seasons. The colour of the sky should correlate with that of the grass, plants and other elements in the landscape.

Watercolour, **Javier Fuentes**

Marine art

STARTING TO PAINT MARINE ART

With marine art, it is almost obligatory to paint the line of the horizon. In fact, it is perhaps the only landscape where it is essential to keep this line as straight as possible and, of course, horizontal.

Maine's rocky shores, **Brienne M. Brown**

La Coruña, **Rubén de Luis**

Marina Real, **Antonio Sánchez Serrano**

DRAWING THE HORIZON IN MARINE ART

There are different ways of drawing a straight line using watercolours. One is to use a ruler. Another is by using masking tape, which you should stick to the paper while it is dry.

248

TECHNIQUE FOR DRAWING THE HORIZON IN MARINE ART

It is possible to produce a straight line using wet watercolours. This procedure involves absorbing wet colour using a strip of adhesive tape, intentionally creating a cut that is as straight as possible.

249

HOW TO POSITION THE HORIZON IN MARINE ART

One of the best ways of positioning the line of the horizon in a seascape is to divide the height of the painting surface into three parts. Position the line of the horizon at the division of the upper or lower third, but never between them, so never in the middle. A seascape with the line of the horizon at the centre of the painting is considered unharmonious.

THE SEA AS THE PROTAGONIST IN MARINE ART

If you want to give protagonism to the sea, position the horizon in the upper section. If, on the other hand, the sky is the protagonist, then choose the lower section.

HOW TO PAINT THE SEA IN MARINE ART

It is essential to consider the perspective of the sea when painting marine art. Remember that the sea and its waves should be painted with proper perspective, unless you want to create visual and aesthetic chaos.

WAVES IN MARINE ART

In a seascape where the onlooker is perpendicular to the line of the horizon, the lines that form the different waves that are successively nearing the shore will also appear horizontal. Conversely, if the onlooker is at an angle to the horizon, these lines will have the same perspective as that of the coastline.

Marina, **Eduardo Marticorena**

Waiting to shove off, **Keene Wilson**

Leaves on the water, **Hsin-I-Kuo**

THE COLOUR OF THE SEA IN MARINE ART

The best way to identify which colours to use when painting the sea is to look at works by old masters.

THE COLOUR PALETTE FOR THE SEA IN MARINE ART

Paint the sea with its own colour palette. While the sea may be blue, in reality, it will permit millions of colours and combinations.

IDENTIFYING COLOURS FOR THE SEA IN MARINE ART

Greens, blues (ultramarine, Prussian, cerulean and cobalt), violets, indigos, ochres, and even oranges, yellows and reds can all be used for the sea. The range of colours is infinite when it comes to painting a seascape.

THE COLOUR OF THE HORIZON IN MARINE ART

Regarding the colours of the horizon in a seascape, you will very often observe how, where the sky touches the line of the horizon, the tones become warmer and lighter. Obviously, there are exceptions, and it is all relative. But, it is essential to observe this detail when painting a seascape.

Cantabrian Sea, **Marene Lasagabaster**

BLUE-GREEN FOR THE SEA IN MARINE ART

The sea has a 'normal colour'. To avoid getting it wrong, it is best to start by painting the sea using a blue-green.

FINISHING THE WAVES ON THE SEA IN MARINE ART

If you are planning to paint foam on the waves, it is essential to avoid using just white. Playing with other colours will add drama and consistency to your work.

West coast glitter, **Ronald Hazell**

WHITE IN MARINE ART

A perfect, opaque body of white is never found in nature because it will always be altered by the dominant colour in the light source it is receiving. Consequently, if the artist uses pure white, without nuances, the resulting painting will be implausible.

260

LIGHT IN MARINE ART

If you want to add highlights to your work, always mix white with a small amount of colour, based on the colour wheel.

Cruz del Mar beach, **Luis Lomelino**

Venetian winter, **Carlos Martín**

261

FINDING THE COLOUR FOR LIGHT IN MARINE ART

Always look for the dominant colour in the source of illumination. That will be the colour from the colour wheel that you should mix with white to create highlights.

262

WASHES IN MARINE ART

When working with large areas, it is best to perform the first wash using a highly transparent tone or colour, to illuminate the white of the paper. This trick is crucial when painting waves on the sea.

MIXING WHITE IN MARINE ART

It is important to remember that Chinese white is a highly opaque colour. It does not work very well when mixed with any other colour. This is why using it to add highlights may produce the opposite effect, that is, make the colour grey instead of illuminating it.

▲

Beach, **Francisco Peral Bárcena**

264

DEPICTING THE MOTION OF THE SEA IN MARINE ART

The motion of the sea is the most important element to capture in any seascape. This can be achieved only by adding each brush-stroke with great care. It is essential to think about the direction and length of each brush-stroke.

265

LIGHT AND DARK IN MARINE ART

Playing with light and dark is a determining factor in achieving volume, luminosity, highlights and shadows. This is a key detail when you paint a seascape.

Morning splendor,
Brienne M. Brown
▼

Nudes

266

SKIN COLOUR IN NUDES

Skin colour can vary considerably depending on the age and origin of the person you are painting. It is therefore important to take this diversity into account when producing your artwork. Observe lighter and darker nuances, and the light, to achieve the most realistic results possible.

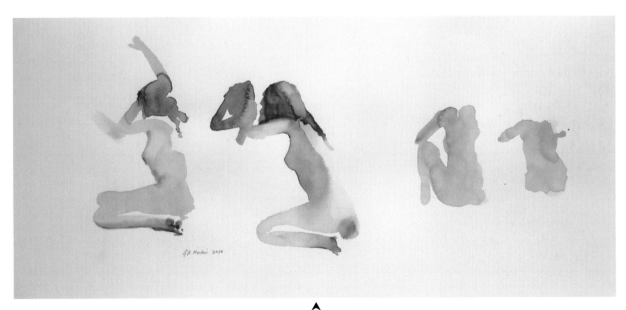

▲
Nude poses, **Gary Korlin**

Skin tone is a determining factor when it comes to painting nudes,
Sylvie Guillot

SKIN TONE IN NUDES

It is vital to identify the base skin tone of the subject you are going to paint. These tones are, generally speaking, pale, black, olive or red. In watercolours, it is best to try to mix the base tone on your palette, by using an appropriate combination of alizarin crimson, raw Sienna, ochre yellow and burnt earth. You will not always need all four colours.

Killer heels, **Pauline Adair**

268

APPLYING SKIN TONE IN NUDES

Test the basic skin tone you have mixed on a piece of waste water-colour paper. Apply it heavily and lightly with your paintbrush, adding water to the brush, to lighten the colour. Adjust the mixture as necessary and concentrate only on the value of the primary tone and the value of the medium tone of the skin.

269

COLOUR PALETTE IN NUDES

Different painters will use different palettes to paint the human figure. While certain colours may reappear, like red and yellow, the possibilities are infinite.

270

LIGHT IN NUDES

When dealing with a light skin tone or when you want to paint illuminated areas, a good mixture is yellow ochre + white + a little vermilion.

◄ *Every painter should have their own colour palette for painting nude figures,* **Mentiradeloro**

271

SHADOW IN NUDES

When dealing with a darker skin tone or zones without much light or that are in shadow, a good option is natural Sienna + vermilion.

Marianna, ► **Sylvie Guillot**

Sleeping figure,
Pauline Adair

Amanda 20 min with drips,
Keene Wilson

272

HIGHLIGHTS
IN NUDES

It is best to avoid using just white for highlights or the places that are receiving the most light. A better option is to try adding yellow ochre or yellow, or any other colour, without worrying whether it is warm or cool, but never white alone.

273

REALIST AND
IMPRESSIONIST NUDES

Skin tones do not vary depending on whether the work is more realistic or more impressionistic. In fact, they stay the same. The only difference is in the brush-stroke.

274

VOLUME
IN NUDES

It is better to be able to control light and dark then capture the exact colour of the skin. In other words, it is more important to portray the volume of the human figure than its colour.

◀ *I am the bad parrot,* **Mentiradeloro**

275

INTENSIFYING SHADOWS IN NUDES

When working with nudes, a good trick is to add a burnt umber tone, to intensify the warm tones.

276

WASHES IN NUDES

Another good trick when painting nudes is to add ultramarine blue or any other cold tone, but one that is very transparent, to cool down the preceding warm washes.

277

TONES WHEN STARTING A NUDE PAINTING

It is best to start painting a nude using medium tones. Subsequently, apply light and shadow at the same time, to define the form and volume of the figure.

278

DETAILS AND ERRORS IN NUDES

Observe the painting carefully, looking at it in a mirror. This way, you will be able to identify details and errors that you perhaps did not observe with your naked eye. Some artists use this technique when they complete the sketch of the nude, before they start adding the watercolour paint.

Whether the painting is realistic or not, when you paint a human nude, skin tone is a key factor,
Gary Korlin

HYPERREALISTIC NUDES

If you are producing a hyperrealistic painting, you will need to have a wide variety of brush sizes and types. It is impossible to paint every aspect of a hyperrealistic painting without the exact brush you need for the work.

CONTRASTS IN NUDES

It is a good idea to practise with different colour contrasts. That is the only way for a painter to find their own harmony.

MOVEMENT IN NUDES

Seven types of contrast have been identified. A useful tip is to try one painting using only pure colours, and another with light greys. This way, you will be able to observe how the colours totally change the sensation of movement.

Figure, **Pauline Adair**

Nude one, **Consuelo Córcoles**
▼

EXERCISE FOR PAINTING A NUDE

A useful exercise is to imagine a nude person lying down, almost asleep, in soft colours and greys. This painting would convey the feeling of peace and stillness. Conversely, if you imagine the same scene in strong, contrasting colours, the work would be more lively. It would look as if the subject were about to move.

Nude study, **Mariló Carranza**

ISSUES WITH COLOUR AND VOLUME IN NUDES

If you are finding it difficult to paint colour and volume, start by painting in grisaille, that is, using a single colour. This way, volume will be the only aspect you will have to think about. You can add colour later.

284

PROPORTION IN NUDES

When working with nudes, particularly in realist painting, proportion is fundamental. Proportion means the size of an object in relation to the other objects around it. The easiest way to achieve good proportion is to learn how to measure.

285

THE HEAD IN NUDES

The best unit of measurement to use when drawing a person (nude or dressed) is the head. The head is neither the biggest nor the smallest part of the body, which means it is a very useful part to compare with other areas of the body.

Nude study 4,
Mariló Carranza ▶

Fruit

LIGHT AND SHADOW WITH FRUIT

Light and shadow play a vital role when it comes to painting fruit. If the light is poor, you lose the essence of the colours, contrast, the effects of depth and shadow.

▲

Juicy fruit, **Jorge Mato Huelves**

Plums, **Manuel Gandullo**

287

NATURAL OR ARTIFICIAL LIGHT WITH FRUIT

It is possible to use natural or artificial light when you paint. The type of light you select will have a direct effect on your colour preparation.

288

NATURAL LIGHT WITH FRUIT

If you are going to use natural light, you should bear in mind the position of the sun. This is because, as the day progresses, the sun changes position, which means the shadows will alter.

289

A PHOTO FOR FRUIT

It is a good idea to take a photo and use it as a point of reference for the shadows on each piece of fruit or your entire composition at a specific moment in the day.

This painting of a strawberry plant was produced using natural light, **David Scheirer**

290

ARTIFICIAL LIGHT WITH FRUIT

Artificial light, unlike natural light, is easier to manipulate and control, since you can move it around, to study the shadows. You can also control its intensity, to analyse how it alters the colours. This way, it will let you better analyse how best to illuminate your work.

LOTS OF FRUIT

If your painting is going to contain lots of fruit, it is best to try with different pieces of fruit in different positions. You can adjust the fruit in question as many times as you think necessary. The objective is always to achieve a composition that is pleasing to the eye.

Lemons,
Lineke Zubieta ➤

Glass dish with fruit, **Jorge Mato Huelves**
⌄

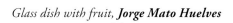

DIFFERENT ANGLES WITH FRUIT

Visualise your work from different angles. Observe it close up and at a distance, until you obtain a composition that is sufficiently balanced and pleasing to the eye. Try to achieve a composition that is attractive for the artist and the onlooker, by playing with the forms and heights of the objects that comprise it.

Original painting where the background merges with the body of the subject,
Luis Lomelino

Apple burst, **Lori Jeremiah**

BACKGROUND
WITH FRUIT

———

The background colour plays a fundamental role in this type of artwork. This is because you can use it to create contrast for all the pieces in your painting.

DIFFERENT BACKGROUNDS
WITH FRUIT

———

There is an enormous variety of backgrounds. You could use a wall, fabric or a piece of paper as your background. Your imagination is another great source of backgrounds. Use your creativity to bring life to any type of background.

DIFFERENT COLOURS
WITH FRUIT

———

It is essential to be conscious of the colour of the objects you are going to paint. Their colour should stand in contrast to the background. Otherwise, you will lose contrast and the effect of depth. So, for instance, if the fruit is red, the background should be a different colour.

It is important for the fruit to rest on a support.

296

SUPPORTING THE FRUIT

Having a support will help you bring life to your painting. Perhaps, the fruit could rest on a table. In this case, it is best to cover the table with a shiny material, which will allow you to create some type of reflection.

297

DYNAMISM WITH FRUIT

Another option for creating dynamism and interest is to use an element to accompany the fruit, like a bowl.

This painting's dynamism comes from the plant's branches,
Jorge Mato Huelves

▲

Painting in which we can see different pieces of fruit with the same placement and tone,
Jorge Mato Huelves

COMPOSITION WITH FRUIT

———

It is important to set up an interesting composition in artworks of this type. One good tip is to create a focal point for your composition, using a large or intricate element, and organise other smaller elements around it.

▲

Creating order when you position the fruit is very important if you want to produce a good composition,
Laurin McCracken

CONTRAST WITH FRUIT

———

It is possible to create a feeling of drama and contrast for an element in the work. So, for instance, you could position a large piece of fruit next to one that is much smaller, or balance the image by using elements of the same size.

HUES WITH FRUIT

A good piece of advice for observing the different hues of a particular fruit is to cut a small rectangle in the centre of a piece of cardboard or paper, to create a viewfinder. This viewfinder will help you explore interesting possibilities for your image, without you having to reorganise the objects in your composition.

VARIETY WITH FRUIT

Variety is a great ally in this type of painting. By playing with different textures and objects, you can enrich your work. Use different combinations of objects made of materials like metal, wood, paper, plastic, stone and glass.

Contrasts give a painting movement and proportion, **Jorge Mato Huelves**

DEPTH WITH FRUIT

If you want to create greater depth in your scene, you could position reflective objects near flat surfaces. Another option is to use colourful objects, to introduce additional colours and partially hide larger objects.

Other juicy fruits, **Jorge Mato Huelves**

▲

Light and shadow finish off pieces,
Laurin McCracken

▲

Juicy fruits on a tray, **Jorge Mato Huelves**

STILL LIFE WITH FRUIT

Fruit is a popular subject for still-life paintings. It is an excellent choice for beginners. You can use fruit to study how light and shadow behave in nature.

STARTING TO WORK WITH FRUIT

It is a good idea to start painting fruit and other still-life subjects, like flowers, before moving on to more complex figures, like people and animals.

EXERCISE WITH FRUIT

A still life with fruit is a good exercise for artists starting to work with watercolours.

Animals

STARTING TO PAINT ANIMALS

Painting animals using watercolours is considered to be quite challenging. Given that this is a realist subject, it is not recommended for beginners, and is more suitable for artists with some experience.

Seeking, **Alarie Tano**

ANIMAL FUR AND HAIR

Animal fur and hair are among the hardest things to paint. Here, texture plays a very important role. The reason why animal fur is one of the hardest textures to depict is because the artist has to show the direction of growth, define the body and muscles of the animal, and portray the different tones their fur adopts in the light.

PROCESS FOR PAINTING ANIMAL FUR

Animal fur should be painted using layers, to represent the successive strands of fur or hair on the animal. You need a special paintbrush to do this.

THE FIRST COLOUR WHEN PAINTING ANIMALS

The first step is to create the background colour for the fur. This can vary, depending on the part of the animal's body.

WHAT TO OBSERVE WHEN PAINTING FUR

It is important to observe the direction of growth, from the roots to the ends, and how long the fur is. All this will determine the length of the brush-stroke.

Wolf study, **Mentiradeloro**

Painting animals in watercolours requires advanced technique, **David Scheirer**

PAINTING THE MUSCLES OF ANIMALS

An animal's musculature is another crucial factor to take into account. This is because it produces movements in the fur and effects of light and shadow on it.

TONES FOR PAINTING ANIMAL FUR

It is a good idea to use different tones of each colour to create a more realistic coat. When the time comes to give life to the shadows, add details in darker tones.

Polar bear, **David Lobenberg**

HOW TO START PAINTING ANIMAL FUR

It is best to start painting fur from the feet and tail and to move upwards, layer by layer, so the layers overlap each other. The final layer, which will be the animal's back, will be the one on the top.

STILL LIFES WITH ANIMALS

Dead animals are considered part of the still-life universe. However, they are much harder to paint than other components of the still life.

Pet portrait, **David Scheirer**
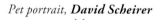

315

ZONES WHEN PAINTING ANIMAL FUR

In zones where you can see the animal's muscles, start the hair shaft where the muscle starts, to mark this part.

316

BRUSH-STROKES WHEN PAINTING ANIMAL FUR

Your brush-strokes should always follow the direction of growth, which means they should get finer at the end of the hair.

The lynx, ***Alarie Tano***

Dog portrait, ***David Scheirer***

317

COMPOSITION WITH ANIMALS

Composition is a key part of painting animals. If you are painting a bird, for instance, you will need to show whether it is flying or sitting on a branch. With domestic animals, you may want to show whether they are inside or outside. This way, you can create interesting plays on colour and contrast.

Attempting to paint animals in their natural surroundings is necessary to achieve a more correct composition, **Lori Jeremiah**

START WITH THE BACKGROUND BEHIND THE ANIMAL

It is best to start with the background. So, for instance, if you are drawing a bird in flight, you would start by painting the sky. Dampen the brush, apply blue paint, and start washing it over the paper, allowing the water to disperse naturally across the surface. Once you have produced this sky wash, you can add more blue, and then clouds.

PAINTING BIRDS

When painting birds, it is a good idea to start with the head. Next, define the shape of the body.

TONES FOR PAINTING BIRDS

Using different colour tones will help you bring out the texture of the bird's feathers. Besides using different tones, you can achieve texture by applying lines of black paint using a very small paintbrush, to depict the layers of feathers.

Cetti's warbler, **Consuelo Córcoles**

IMPROVING PARTS OF A BIRD

A good way to improve the quality of feathers that stand out over the layers created using the fine black lines is to wet a brush and blend the paint on each feather, to grade the colour.

PAINTING PARTS OF A FISH

If you want to paint the scales on a fish, it is best to choose a light tone for larger spaces and a darker one for details. This way, you will create better texture in your work.

PAINTING THE BACKGROUND BEHIND A FISH

When painting fish, it is a good idea to paint the background lighter than the subject (the fish). This way, you will create good contrast, with the animal and its details standing out.

▲
Birds,
David Scheirer

Fish, ➤
David Lobenberg

PERSPECTIVE WITH FISH

If the perspective in the painting of the fish is from above, certain aspects, like reflections on the back of the fish or its eyes, will be of central importance.

▲

Angel fish, **Lori Jeremiah**

325

▼

WATER FOR THE FISH

Water is the second most important element when painting a fish. It is worth playing with its different hues. Light, shadow, movement and colour play a primary role when creating an artwork capable of conveying sensations.

◄ *Fish,* **Lineke Zubieta**

Flowers

STARTING TO PAINT FLOWERS

A good way to start a watercolour painting of flowers is by creating a sketch with simple, soft lines, without much definition, to serve as a guide.

This painting uses simple lines,
Juan Falcón

A MODEL FOR PAINTING FLOWERS

Remember that while you can start with a natural model, the final result does not have to be an exact copy of it. In fact, the most feasible and probable outcome is that the final result will be the painter's interpretation of the flower they are looking at.

COLOURS FOR PAINTING FLOWERS

Colours are a fundamental part of working with flowers. To create the base, it is best to opt for a medium tone. So, for instance, if you are working with a red flower, the base should not be an especially dark or light red.

SHADOWS WITH FLOWERS

When painting the shadows on a flower, it is best to use the darkest colour in the range you are working with. Remember that the darkest parts will be between the petals and in the areas nearest the stem.

LIGHT WITH FLOWERS

It is important to block out areas of light for the flowers. You can leave these without any paint on them. If you find this difficult, use masking fluid.

LEAVES ON FLOWERS

Leaves are a very important part of painting flowers. Before starting to paint them, a good tip is to use a separate piece of paper, to play with different types of green, until you achieve the correct tones.

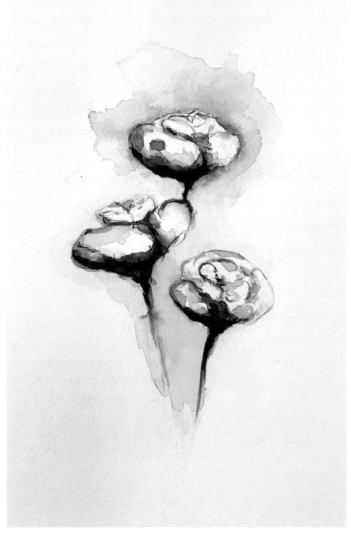

◄ *Poppies,* **Domantas Didžiapetris**

GREEN IN THE LEAVES OF FLOWERS

When painting leaves, start by applying the lightest green. Let the first layer dry a little and then apply the second lightest tone. Here, apply another layer in the same colour and, while the paint is still wet, incline the paper slightly, to allow the paint to slide to the tip of the leaf. This way, one part will remain darker.

FLOWERS IN STILL LIFES

Flowers are considered a variant of the still life. Like fruit, they are ideal for people who are just starting to paint with watercolours.

Flowers study 2, **Karin Johannesson**

Example of the grid method.

USING GRIDS WITH FLOWERS

The grid method is one option that can help you paint a flower. It involves drawing a grid over your reference image and then drawing another grid, with equal proportions, on the surface you are going to paint on. Next, draw what you can see in each of the squares on the original image, one by one, until you form the complete image.

Flower study, **Juan Falcón** ►

WATERCOLOURS WITH FLOWERS

It is important to remember that the technique for working with watercolours is a little harder to master than the technique for other types of paint, like oils. This is because the artist must be clear on which colour they are going to use from the outset. So, it is vital you identify the colour of the flower before you start painting it.

336

LIGHT AND SHADOW WITH FLOWERS

Light and shadow play a crucial role in this type of work. You can use natural or artificial light. If you are working with natural light, it is important to take different factors into account, like the time of day or season. This way, you will bring more realism to your flower.

337

ROSES: THE PIONEERS

Roses are one of the most painted flowers. The petals of a rose are small. So, there are sharp transitions from light to dark. The artist can create lines of darkness and light where they join.

▲

Flowers, **Karin Johannesson**

164

ARTIFICIAL LIGHT WITH FLOWERS

Using artificial light for your flowers will help you create much more controlled environments, which are easier to paint.

The light and shadow
on the flowers produce
the plant's outlines,
Ayşe Eylül Sönmez

LIGHT AND SHADOW WITH PETALS

Light and shadow on the petals play an essential role in this type of work. You must make sure that the paint is sufficiently light to allow you to add soft shadows, to depict the contours and shadows of other petals.

Poppy flowers,
Domantas Didžiapetris

A MODEL FOR PAINTING FLOWERS

Remember that while you can start with a natural model, the final result does not have to be an exact copy of it. In fact, the most feasible and probable outcome is that the final result will be the painter's interpretation of the flower they are looking at.

You can often make the stem a
base for the rest of the flower,
Tito Fornasiero

THE STEM AND LEAVES

It is useful to regard the stem as a
cylinder, and the leaves below the
flower as green petals. The leaves
should appear less translucent
than the petals.

MODELS AND PHOTOGRAPHS WITH FLOWERS

If you are going to work from
a model or photograph, check
every petal, comparing it against
the original. This will help you
find details you have missed, like
highlights and shadows, and you
will be able to add them.

Vertical gardens, ▶
Juan Falcón

Same colour,
different tones,
Karin Johannesson

LIGHT TONES FOR FLOWERS

It is important to make sure the paint is sufficiently light to allow you to add soft shadows, to depict the contours and shadows of the different petals.

344

SUBJECT AND BACKGROUND WITH FLOWERS

As in any other still life, the relationship between the subject and its background is fundamental. In order for the subject to stand out, in this case, the flower, you will need a simple background that does not distract from it.

345

TEXTURES WITH FLOWERS

One good way of enriching a painting of a flower is to use different textures. This can be achieved by including different flowers, or other elements, like a tablecloth or vase.

Pink poppies, **Karin Johannesson**

167

Portraits

STARTING TO PAINT PORTRAITS

The composition of the portrait is fundamental. When the portrait is the central focus, it is important that no other point should rival it. To achieve this, the artist can follow the basic concepts of the rule of thirds or the golden ratio.

Profile, ***Ángela Barreiro Ruiz***

PROPORTIONS WHEN PAINTING PORTRAITS

It is essential to respect proportion. Beginners will often increase the size of certain elements, such as the eyes or mouth, and reduce the size of others, like the ears, neck, forehead or hair.

MODELS FOR PAINTING PORTRAITS

If you are going to work with models, it is a good idea to capture their image down to the shoulders. This way, you will be able to better reflect the personality and attitude of the subject.

AN IMPORTANT POINT ABOUT PORTRAITS

The gaze is a very important part of any portrait. In a profile or three-quarter portrait, it is important to leave the largest section of 'air' on the side where the person is looking. But, you should also be careful to leave sufficient space above the head, to make sure your composition is balanced.

MORE REALISM IN PORTRAITS

To produce a good portrait, the artist will need to soften the contours of the shadows, to make them more realistic. This effect is easy to achieve, by applying the colour and then passing a clean damp brush over the edges of the area in question.

THE MOUTH IN PORTRAITS

To paint the mouth, apply more-or-less-diluted brush-strokes, depending on how much light is reflected. To create shine, leave an area unpainted at the centre of the lower lip.

Wild things, **Robyn Pees**

EYES IN PORTRAITS

If you want to make the eyes look rounder, highlight the upper eyelid and add subtle shadow to the lower one.

PARTS OF THE EYES IN PORTRAITS

It is crucial to define the lower eyelid. This will help the eye appear well placed and avoid it looking as if it is 'floating'.

EXPRESSIVE EYES IN PORTRAITS

To create expressive eyes, you have to clearly define the line where the upper eyelid folds when the eye is open.

LIGHT AND SHADOW IN PORTRAITS

Observe and capture, with detail and dedication, the forms, lights and shadows inside the eye. This trick will give the gaze much more depth.

Girl,
David Lobenberg

Consume,
Ali Cavanaugh

THE SKIN IN PORTRAITS

Colour mixtures to depict the skin in a portrait can and should vary from artist to artist and work to work.

TONES ON THE FOREHEAD IN PORTRAITS

There are several details that do not tend to vary across different portraits. One example is that ochre tones will predominate on the forehead. Another is that cool tones linked to the violets will normally be used in the eye area.

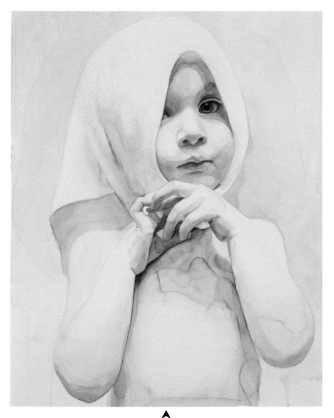

In a dream, **Ali Cavanaugh**

358

THE CHEEKS IN PORTRAITS

Another constant in portraits can be observed in the cheek area (generally associated with pinks), on the nose (where there tends to be more reds or oranges), and on the jaw, where artists will often use grey tones for women and green ones for men.

SKIN TONE IN PORTRAITS

Skin tone is portrayed by interchanging warm and cool tones. A good method to avoid forgetting this is to paint the entire face using only warm colours and then work with just cool tones, adding them only to the areas where they are supposed to be.

Blue blood blues, **Guilhem Sals**
⌄

WHITE IN PORTRAITS

Never use just white for highlights or the places that are receiving the most light. Add other tones, like yellow ochre, yellow, or any other colour (normally the colour of the light illuminating the face) without worrying whether they are warm or cool.

SKIN TONE IN PORTRAITS

Skin tone will not vary based on whether the portrait is more realistic or impressionistic. It will be the same. The difference resides in how the artist uses the paintbrush, to create more or less blurring.

LIGHT AND DARK IN PORTRAITS

Becoming proficient in using light and dark will help you capture the exact colours of the skin. In other words, it is more important to portray the volume of the face than its colour.

Freckle, **Guilhem Sals**

Deep blue, **Mentiradeloro**

363

LIGHT TONES FIRST IN PORTRAITS

Start your portrait with light tones and progressively darken it.

364

THE BACKGROUND IN PORTRAITS

It is important to bear in mind that the tones or colours in the background are normally reflected at the top of the cheeks.

365

CLOTHES IN PORTRAITS

The colour of the clothes will be reflected on the chin and the lower part of the jaw.

Contributor Index

Alarie Tano (Simon Schmidt)
alarie.de
p. 13, 154, 157

Ali Cavanaugh
alicavanaugh.com
p. 6, 170, 171

Ángela Barreiro Ruiz
anbarrui.wixsite.com
p. 168

Antonio Sánchez Serrano
acuarelassanchezserrano.blogspot.com
p. 75, 105, 113, 128, 131, 133

Ayşe Eylül Sönmez
eylulaysesonmez.blogspot.com.es
p. 7, 80, 94, 114, 165

Brienne M. Brown
briennembrown.com
p. 84, 123, 124, 132, 138

Carlos Martín
carlosmartin-arte.blogspot.com.es
p. 67, 114, 137

Charles Reid
charlesreidart.com
p. 109

Christina Papagianni
xrispapag@hotmail.com
p. 103

Chung-Wei Chien
chienchungwei.com
p. 49, 53, 54, 72, 77, 83, 85, 87, 92, 95, 96

Colin Maxwell
colinmaxwell.net
p. 95, 100, 115, 120

Consuelo Córcoles
consuelocorcoles.es
p. 73, 119, 125, 144, 158

Dámaso Carrillo
pinturasdamasocarrillo.blogspot.com.es
p. 116

David Lobenberg
lobenbergart.com
p. 107, 108, 156, 159, 170

David Scheirer
dswatercolors.com
p. 79, 117, 147, 155, 156, 157, 159

Domantas Didžiapetris
ddi.lt
p. 102, 162, 165

Eduardo Marticorena
edmarticorenart.wordpress.com
p. 112, 134

Francisco Peral Bárcena
franciscoperalbarcena.blogspot.com.es
p. 82, 118, 130, 138

Gary Korlin
garykorlin.com
p. 139, 143

Guilhem Sals
guilhem-watercolor.tumblr.com
p. 101, 109, 172, 173

Hsin-I Kuo
kuoart.com
p. 29, 31, 32, 33, 34, 35, 39, 43, 45, 63, 64, 65, 68, 69, 71, 72, 85, 88, 92, 93, 96, 135

Ian Ramsay
ianramsay.blogspot.com.es
p. 61, 64, 73, 76, 78

Irina Sztukowski
irinasztukowski.com
p. 62

Isabel Mancebo
isabelmancebobalda@gmail.com
p. 102

Javier Fuentes
acuarelas-javierfuentes.blogspot.com.es
p. 118, 121, 125, 127, 131

Jean Gill
jeankgill.com
p. 77, 81

Joan Iaconetti
joaniaconetti.com
p. 39, 93, 97

Jorge Mato Huelves
artemato.blogspot.com.es
p. 146, 148, 150, 151, 152, 153

Juan Falcón
falconespaciocreativo.wordpress.com
p. 161, 164, 166

Karin Johannesson
karinjohannesson.com
p. 58, 91, 115, 163, 164, 167

Keene Wilson
keenewilson.com
p. 135, 142

Kwan Yuen Tam
kytam.com
p. 46

Laurin McCracken
lauringallery.com
p. 32, 34, 44, 45, 151, 153

Linda Doll
lindadoll.com
p. 54, 55, 60, 81

Líneke Zubieta
linekezubieta.com
p. 47, 89, 111, 148, 160

Lori Jeremiah
lorijeremiah.com
p. 88, 149, 158, 160

Luis Lomelino
lomelinoacuarelista.blogspot.com.es
p. 104, 111, 127, 128, 137, 149

Manuel Gandullo
pintoresgallegos.com/gandullo/paisajes.html
p. 5, 129, 130, 147

Marene Lasagabaster
marenelasagabaster.wordpress.com
p. 119, 136

Mariló Carranza
marilocarranza.blogspot.com.es
p. 145

Matej Jan
matejjan.com
p. 59-75

Mentiradeloro
mentiradeloro.wordpress.com
p. 141, 142, 155, 173

Pauline Adair
paulineadair.com
p. 112, 140, 142, 144

Robyn Pees
behance.net/rcbynn
p. 101, 169

Ronald Hazell
ronhazell.com
p. 110, 129, 136

Rubén de Luis
rubendeluis.com.es
p. 133

Sylvie Guillot
sylvieguillot.com
p. 117, 140, 141

Tan Suz Chiang
tansuzchiang.com
p. 74, 82, 94

Tayete Garcia
tayete.blogspot.com.es
p. 70, 90, 107, 110

Tito Fornasiero
artmajeur.com/es/art-gallery/tito-fornasiero
p. 86, 98, 126, 166

Vinita Pappas
vinitapappas.com
p. 105, 121, 126

Further reading

Brambilla Daniela, *Human Figure Drawing: Drawing Gestures, Postures and Movements* (2015), Promopress

Colombo Giovanni and Vigliotti Giuseppe, *Drawing the Human Head: Anatomy, Expressions, Emotions and Feelings* (2017), Promopress

Elizegi Rebeka, *Collage Therapy: Cutting Out Stress* (2016), Promopress

Escandell Victor, *The Resourceful Artist: Exploring Mixed Media and Collage Techniques* (2017), Promopress